Robin Dunne is a barrister at Hardwicke specialising in costs and litigation funding, having focused exclusively on this area of law since call. He appears at every level of hearing, up to and including the Court of Appeal.

He was called to the bar in 2002 and was an employed barrister and partner in a City of London firm of solicitors before independent practice.

His practice includes between the parties and solicitor and client disputes as well as professional negligence claims involving solicitors, particularly where the dispute involves issues relating to costs. He has appeared in many of the leading cases relating to solicitor and client costs.

www.hardwicke.co.uk

A Practical Guide to Solicitor and Client Costs

2nd Edition

A Practical Guide to Solicitor and Client Costs
2nd Edition

Robin Dunne BA (hons), Pg. Dip
of the Middle Temple, Barrister
Hardwicke Chambers, London

Law Brief Publishing

Published 2018 by Law Brief Publishing, an imprint of Law Brief Publishing Ltd
30 The Parks
Minehead
Somerset
TA24 8BT

www.lawbriefpublishing.com

Paperback: 978-1-913715-39-7

PREFACE TO THE
SECOND EDITION

There would be many periods in the 46 years since the enactment of the Solicitors Act when a book concerning solicitor and client costs would not need updating for many years. The fact that this edition is required two years after the first is testament to the continued growth of solicitor and client disputes.

This edition has been updated to include a number of important cases reported since the first edition. It has also been expanded to include commentary on issues which have arisen since that time.

Despite the book's slightly larger size, the intention that it should remain a short and practical guide remains.

The law is stated as at 1st July 2020.

Robin Dunne
July 2020

PREFACE TO THE
FIRST EDITION

The solicitors' profession is highly regulated. Their remuneration is no exception.

It would be difficult to think of another profession where the questions of how and when the professional may recover their fees is so tightly regulated by statute, codes of conduct and common law. If the various rules and statutes were simple and easily understood that would cause few problems; however, this is far from the case.

There has been court oversight of lawyer's fees since the thirteenth century. The precursor to the modern statutory regulation of solicitors is the Solicitors Act 1843 (replacing the 'Act for the better Regulation of Attorneys and Solicitors', 1729). From this point the statutory regime was altered and updated regularly with the following enactments[1]:

- The Attorneys' and Solicitors' Act 1870
- The Solicitors' Remuneration Act 1881
- The General Order 1883
- The Solicitors' Remuneration Act General Order 1920
- The Solicitors Act 1932
- The Solicitors' Remuneration (Gross Sum) Order 1934
- The Solicitors Remuneration Order 1953
- The Solicitors (Amendment) Act 1956
- The Solicitors Act 1957

---

1 For those interested in the rules that were enacted with each new act and some of the case law which followed, Ward LJ sets out the detail in Ralph Hume Garry (a firm) v Gwillim - [2002] EWCA Civ 1500 from [16]- [44]. In his own words he was required to 'trawl' through 273 years of statutes and case law (an exercise he found to be an "interesting, if not entirely satisfactory experience"),

The current Act governing the remuneration of solicitors is the Solicitors Act 1974 (as amended) but the changes have not stopped there. When considering the practice of solicitor and client costs one must take The Courts and Legal Services Act 1990 (as amended by the Legal Aid and Punishment of Offenders Act 2012 – 'LASPO') into account as well as The Solicitors' (non-contentious business) Remuneration Order 2009.

The list above does not include the multiple regulations and SIs which provide the rules for various types of retainer.

Then there is the SRA's Code of Conduct and the Solicitors Accounts Rules.

Finally, there is extensive case law governing the solicitor and client relationship, much of it from Victorian times.

It is no wonder that solicitors, clients and those who advise them find this area of the law complex and esoteric. The purpose of this short book is to explain briefly the main issues which arise during disputes between solicitor and client. The parts of the book deal firstly with retainers, estimates and bills (statue bills and interim statute bills) and then set out the rules and procedures relating to assessing solicitor's costs. Finally, Chapter Seven deals with alternatives to the assessment process.

The intention is that anyone who finds themselves involved with a solicitor and client costs dispute will be able to find the answers to questions quickly and clearly. Whether I have succeeded is left to the reader.

I hope the following will find the book useful:

Solicitors: For trainee solicitors or those newly qualified this book should give them a sound understanding of the general principles involved in a solicitor's remuneration. Appreciating the issues will hopefully avoid many of the problems that frequently arise when the relationship between client and solicitor breaks down.

For more experienced solicitors I hope that this modest book will allow them to quickly and easily look up the main topics that arise where there is a dispute over fees. I would also hope the chapters on the assessment process would provide practical guidance as to how and when they may recover their fees.

Clients: While this book is primarily written for legal professionals it will be of use to clients who have questions about their solicitor's fees and wish to understand how to go about challenging them.

Costs Lawyers and Counsel who are advising or acting in solicitor and client disputes.

Non-specialist judges who require a short guide to solicitor and client costs.

The law is stated as at 1st May 2018.

Robin Dunne
May 2018

A NOTE ON TERMINOLOGY

Readers will note that in many of the older cases cited the courts use the word 'taxation' rather than 'assessment.' Costs Judges are also referred to as 'Taxing Masters'. The words mean exactly the same thing and the new terminology is used throughout this book. Where a judge uses the old terminology in judgments this is left unchanged.

Throughout this book 'the Act' refers to the Solicitors Act 1974 (as amended).

CPR refers to the Civil Procedure Rules.

PD means the Practice Direction relating to the CPR.

The SRA Code of Conduct refers to the version approved in May 2018 (and available at www.sra.org.uk).

The SCCO refers to the Senior Courts Costs Office, a part of the High Court where specialist costs judges sit.

TABLE OF CASES

CONTENTS

CHAPTER ONE
THE RETAINER

Introduction

1.1. The contract of retainer between solicitor and client governs their relationship. However, the relationship is tightly regulated, both in terms of the Act and the Code of Conduct but also due to common law.

1.2. Arrangements for remuneration between solicitors and their clients can broadly be put into two categories: those which require the client to pay the fees whatever occurs and those which are contingent upon a specified outcome (a contingency agreement).

1.3. Dividing the categories further, there are four main types of retainer:

(i) A private retainer: A standard retainer whereby the client agrees with the solicitor to pay fees whatever the outcome of the case

(ii) A contentious or non-contentious business agreement: An agreement that complies with s.57-63 of the Act (which can be a contingency agreement)

(iii) A Conditional Fee Agreement (CFA): A contingency agreement with the client that provides that the fees will only be payable in certain circumstances, for example, if the case is won the fees are paid but if lost no costs can be recovered from the client. In some circumstances a success fee is payable by the client in addition out of his damages.

(iv) A Damages Based Agreement (DBA): Another type of contingency agreement where the fees are only payable if a specified event occurs- for example a retainer whereby the client agrees to pay the solicitor a fixed percentage of their damages if the case is won (and nothing if the case is lost).

Written or Oral?

1.4. A private retainer can be in writing, be agreed orally or implied by conduct. Lang J has stated:

> "In my judgment, the giving of instructions by a client to a solicitor constitutes the solicitor's retainer by that client. It is not essential that the retainer is in writing. It may be oral. It may be implied by the conduct of the parties in the particular case."[1]

1.5. Despite the above, a retainer should always be in writing. It is a foolhardy solicitor who relies upon an oral agreement or conduct to assert their right to fees, not least because, where there is a dispute, the client's interpretation of an oral retainer is likely to be preferred. As Denning LJ put it[2]:

> "On this question of retainer, I would observe that where there is a difference between a solicitor and his client on it, the courts have said for the last hundred years or more that the word of the client is to be preferred to the word of the solicitor, or, at any rate, more weight is to be given to it... The reason is plain. It is because the client is ignorant and the solicitor is, or should be, learned. If the solicitor does not take the precaution of getting a written retainer, he has only himself to thank for being at variance with his client over it and must take the consequences."

1.6. The other types of retainer must be in writing. The table below shows where the requirement that they be reduced to a written document is set out:

---

1 Fladgate LLP v Harrison [2012] EWHC 67 (QB) at [39]

2 Griffiths v Evans [1953] 2All ER 1364

CFA	The Courts and Legal Services Act 1990 (as amended) s.58(3)
Contentious Business Agreement	The Act s.59(1)
Non-Contentious Business Agreement	The Act s.57(3)
Damages Based Agreement	The Courts and Legal Services Act 1990 (as amended) s.58AA(4)

Complaints

1.7. The Legal Services Board requires that solicitors tell clients in writing at the time they are instructed about their firm's complaints procedure including how to complain and to whom any compliant should be addressed to. The SRA Code of Conduct 2018 states that solicitors must[3]:

> "ensure that clients are informed in writing at the time of engagement about:
> 1. their right to complain to you about your services and your charges;
> 2. how a complaint can be made and to whom; and
> 3. any right they have to make a complaint to the Legal Ombudsman and when they can make any such complaint."

1.8. Further guidance is contained within the Code at 8.4-8.5.

Cancellation of Contracts Regulations

1.9. In certain circumstances (depending on the place and the manner in which the retainer is agreed) a solicitor must provide written notice of the client's right to cancel the agreement without incurring a liability.

---

3   At 8.3

1.10. If the written notification of the right to cancel is required but not given then the contract is unenforceable.[4]

1.11. The requirement to provide this information is contained within two sets of regulations[5]. Each apply to different time periods:

(i) Consumer Contracts (Information, Cancellation and Additional Charges) Regulations 2013 apply to retainers made on or after 13th June 2014.[6]

(ii) The Cancellation of Contracts made in a Consumer's Home or Place of Work Regulations 2008 apply where the contract was made on or after 1st October 2008.[7]

Consumer?

1.12. S.4 of the 2013 regulations define a consumer thus:

"consumer" means an individual acting for purposes which are wholly or mainly outside that individual's trade, business, craft or profession"

1.13. The 2008 regulations uses the same definition, albeit in slightly different language:

"consumer" means a natural person who in making a contract to which these Regulations apply is acting for purposes which can be regarded as outside his trade or profession;"

When do the 2013 regulations apply?

1.14. The regulations apply to three circumstances:

---

4   Cox v Woodlands Manor Care Home [2015] EWCA Civ 415

5   Prior to 2008 the 1987 regulations applied. These are not considered within this book.

6   www.legislation.gov.uk/uksi/2013/3134/made

7   www.legislation.gov.uk/uksi/2008/1816/contents/made

(i) An 'on premises' contract: where the agreement is made at the solicitor's office

(ii) An 'off premises' contract: where there is a personal attendance outside the solicitor's office

(iii) A contract made at distance: where the solicitor and client agree the contract using solely communication at distance (i.e. via the telephone or the internet)

<u>When do the 2008 regulations apply?</u>

1.15. Per s.5 the regulations apply where the agreement is made:

(a) during a visit by the trader to the consumer's home or place of work, or to the home of another individual;

(b) during an excursion organised by the trader away from his business premises; or

(c) after an offer made by the consumer during such a visit or excursion

<u>What are the requirements under the regulations?</u>

2008 regulations:

1.16. The solicitor must provide the client with written notice of his right to cancel the contract. This must be given[8]:

(i) If (a) or (b) above apply: at the time the contract is made or

(ii) If (c) above applies: the notice must be given at the time the offer is made by the consumer.

1.17. The regulations at s.7(3) set out the information to be included.

1.18. The time period for cancellation (the cooling off period) is seven days starting with the date of receipt of the notice of the right to can-

---

8 S.7(2)

cel.[9] Unless the client has requested in writing that the provision of services starts before the cooling off period ends they will not be liable for any fees incurred during this time.[10]

2013 regulations

1.19. The 2013 regulation mirror those above. The solicitor is required to provide written notice of the right of the client to cancel the contract. The normal cooling off period is fourteen days after the day the agreement was made.[11]

1.20. The information required is extensive. For agreements made at the solicitor's office the information is set out within schedule one of the act. For off premises or agreements made at a distance the required information is set out within schedule two.

Consumer Protection

1.21. Clients are protected against the imposition of unfair terms within retainers. For retainers signed prior to 1st October 2015 "The Unfair Terms in Consumer Contracts Regulations 1999[12]" apply.

1.22. Reg. 5 provides:

> *"(1) A contractual term which has not been individually negotiated shall be regarded as unfair[13] if, contrary to the requirement of good faith, it causes a significant imbalance in the parties' rights and obligations arising under the contract, to the detriment of the consume."*

---

9 S.2

10 S.8 and 9

11 S.30

12 http://www.legislation.gov.uk/uksi/1999/2083/contents/made

13 For factors to be taken into account in assessing whether a term is unfair, see reg. 6.

1.23. If a term is found to be unfair then it will not bind the client. However, the finding of an unfair term is not fatal to the entire retainer. Rather, per reg 8.2:

> *"The contract shall continue to bind the parties if it is capable of continuing in existence without the unfair term."*

1.24. For those retainers entered into on or after 1ˢᵗ October 2015, Part 2 of the "Consumer Rights Act 2015"[14] applies.

1.25. The definition of an unfair term at s.62(4) is almost identical to that under the 1999 regulations:

> *"A term is unfair if, contrary to the requirement of good faith, it causes a significant imbalance in the parties' rights and obligations under the contract to the detriment of the consumer."*

1.26. Schedule 2 to the legislation contains a list of terms which may be considered unfair.

1.27. As with the previous regulations, a term which is found to be unfair will not bind the client (although the client can choose to rely upon it if they wish).

Increases in the hourly rate

1.28. If the retainer provides for remuneration by reference to an hourly rate the solicitor will usually want to allow for increases as time passes. If the solicitor wishes to do so then, as a matter of contract, the retainer must provide for this and set out the time period and mechanism by which the increases will take effect.[15]

An Entire Contract

1.29. Save where the retainer provides otherwise, or in limited circumstances[16], an agreement between solicitor and client will be an entire retainer. This has important implications for the solicitor because he will

---

14 http://www.legislation.gov.uk/ukpga/2015/15/section/62/enacted

15 A yearly revision corresponding with RPI/CPI is the simplest method of doing so.

only be able to charge for fees where the entirety of his obligations under the contract are discharged. Walker J put it thus[17]:

> "A solicitor's retainer is an example of what, although known as an "entire contract", is perhaps better described as involving an "entire obligation": a solicitor can generally only claim remuneration when all work has been completed, or when there is a natural break. That, however, is subject to any agreement to the contrary" [10]

1.30. Lord Esher MR in his well-known exposition of the principle said this:

> "When a man goes to a solicitor and instructs him for the purpose of bringing or defending such an action, he does not mean to employ the solicitor to take one step, and then give him fresh instructions to take another step, and so on; he instructs the solicitor as a skilled person to act for him in the action, to take all the necessary steps in it, and to carry it on to the end. If the meaning of the retainer is that the solicitor is to carry on the action to the end, it necessarily follows that the contract of the solicitor is an entire contract - that is, a contract to take all the steps which are necessary to bring the action to a conclusion."[18]

1.31. The issue of entire retainers is considered further at 1.141 below (termination of retainers) and in Chapter Four (interim statute bills).

Naming the Client and Opponent

1.32. In contentious business care should be taken when naming the parties. On a between the parties assessment paying parties frequently take the point that the retainer does not name the correct defendant and therefore does not cover the action. There are a number of first instance decisions involving CFAs where naming the wrong defendant has led to costs being disallowed.

16 A retainer that provides that a solicitor is to act generally for a client is unlikely to be an entire contract, for the obvious reason that it is open ended: Warmingtons v McMurray [1937] 1 All ER 562 see also where there is a natural break (considered in Chapter Four)

17 Vlamaki v Sookias & Sookias [2015] EWHC 3334 (QB)

18 Underwood, Son and Piper v Lewis [1894] 2 QB 306 at 310

1.33. If the identity of a party is unclear then care should be taken. The retainer could provide that it covers:

> "Your claim against X (and any other party that is brought into the proceedings or any party which becomes liable, either by agreement or an order of the court, to pay You damages or costs in relation to Your claim)."

Restrictions on Recovery

1.34. There may be statutory restrictions on the amount of fees recoverable under various types of retainer (for example, the maximum allowable success fee under a CFA or a maximum percentage payable under a DBA). However, of general application to contentious work in county court claims is the restriction under s.74(3) of the Act. This states:

> "The amount which may be allowed on the assessment of any costs or bill of costs in respect of any item relating to proceedings in the county court shall not, except in so far as rules of court may otherwise provide, exceed the amount which could have been allowed in respect of that item as between party and party in those proceedings, having regard to the nature of the proceedings and the amount of the claim and of any counterclaim."

1.35. The CPR at 46.9(2) provides:

> "Section 74(3) of the Solicitors Act 19746 applies unless the solicitor and client have entered into a written agreement which expressly permits payment to the solicitor of an amount of costs greater than that which the client could have recovered from another party to the proceedings."19

1.36. This is a much overlooked provision but is of wide ranging effect. In essence, if a solicitor has not expressly agreed in a written agreement (an oral retainer will not be enough) that the client can be charged more than could have been recovered between the parties the difference will not be recoverable.

---

19 It is not yet established whether there needs to be 'informed consent' (see Chapter Six) in respect of this rule. At the time of writing the High Court was considering the point in the case of *Belsner v CAM Legal Services Limited.*

1.37. With the introduction of fixed costs for a huge swathe of county court matters this provision has become hugely important. It is almost inevitable that fixed costs recovered from the opponent will not cover the actual amount of work undertaken. Failure to agree in writing that the difference can be recovered on a solicitor and client basis will cause the solicitor to lose out.

1.38. This does not simply apply to cases which are won (and costs re-covered from the other side). If the case is lost then, in the absence of agreement, the solicitor is limited to the potential between the parties costs when billing their client for the work done.

Contentious and Non-Contentious Business Agreements

1.39. Why would a solicitor wish to enter into a contentious or non-contentious business agreement? There are two advantages; certainty as to the fees (which is of benefit to both solicitor and client) and, of great benefit to the solicitor, the potential for curtailing the client's rights to assessment under the Act.

1.40. Where a client successfully argues that a retainer is not a valid business agreement the restrictions as to challenging the costs will not apply. In those circumstances the costs will be assessed in the usual way on the normal basis (depending upon whether they are contentious or non-contentious costs[20]).

1.41. A non-contentious business agreement must comply with the Act at s.57. Contentious business agreements are dealt with at s. 59-63 of the Act.

Contentious or non-contentious?

1.42. The Act defines the two types of work thus[21]:

- Contentious Business means:

---

20 See Chapter Six

21 S.87

"business done, whether as solicitor or advocate, in or for the purposes of proceedings begun before a court or before an arbitrator . . ., not being business which falls within the definition of non–contentious or common form probate business contained in section 128 of the Senior Courts Act 1981"

- Non-Contentious Business means:

  "any business done as a solicitor which is not contentious business as defined by this subsection"

1.43. Thus, any work undertaken 'in or for the purposes of proceedings' begun before a court or an arbitrator is contentious business. If proceedings are issued then the work is clearly contentious. If work is done before proceedings are issued they are non-contentious.

1.44. Once the matter becomes issued then the work previously undertaken is retrospectively turned into contentious business.

1.45. Non-contentious business will ordinary be easily identifiable. It would include much commercial, contract and private client work (for example conveyancing). Obviously where the subject of the work is usually non-contentious (probate for example) but becomes litigated (in contested probate proceedings) that would make the work contentious.

1.46. Work undertaken in tribunals[22] has traditionally been considered non-contentious. It is not clear whether that is still the case. If a point turns on this issue then specialist advice should be sought.

Requirement of business agreements

Non-contentious

1.47. The agreement must be in writing and signed by the client or by his agent.[23] It can be retrospective in effect.[24]

---

22 Defined in the Tribunals, Courts and Enforcement Act 2007

23 S.57(3)

24 S.57(1)

1.48. The Act sets out that the terms of remuneration may provide for payment by[25]:

- a gross sum or fixed amount
- an hourly rate
- by commission or a percentage
- by a salary

1.49. The agreement may include or exclude disbursements.

Contentious

1.50. The agreement must be in writing[26] and can include payment by:

- a gross sum or fixed amount
- an hourly rate or salary that is higher or lower than the solicitor would otherwise be entitled to[27]

Certainty

1.51 In *Chamberlain v Boodle & King (a firm)*[28] Denning LJ held that a business agreement

> "...*must be sufficiently specific, so as to tell the client what he is letting himself in for by way of costs.*"

1.52. In *Chamberlain* the court found that the agreement was not sufficiently certain. Denning LJ commented:

> "*It seems to me that the letters in this case do not give the client the least idea of what he is letting himself in for. As counsel for Mr Chamberlain said to us, there is a broad band of many uncertainties. Take, for instance, the rate. It certainly seems high enough to me. It*

25 S.57(2)

26 Denning LJ has found that a contentious business agreement can be contained in letters- Chamberlain v Boodle & King (a firm) - [1982] 3 All ER 188 at [191]

27 S.59(1)

28 [1982] 3 All ER 188

is £60 to £80 an hour. What rate is to be charged? And for what partner? Of what standard? Then £30 to £45 an hour for associates who may be involved. Which legal executives? Of what standard? Which associates? Does it include the typists? That is one of the broad bands which is left completely uncertain by this agreement. Then there is the hourly rate. That must depend on the skill and expertise of the individual partner or associate. A skilled partner can do the work in half the time of a slow partner. Is the client to be charged double the rate because a slow partner has been put on the case? These rates per hour are over a pound a minute. It would seem that there must be a very good system of timing, almost by stopwatch, if that is to be the rate of payment."

1.53. In conclusion, Denning LJ found:

"…that this is not an agreement as to remuneration at all. It is simply an indication of the rate of charging on which the solicitors propose to make up their bill."

1.54. In *Wilson v The Specter Partnership and others*[29] Mann J also stated that:

"The essence of a CBA is certainty. The parties to the CBA define how the client will be charged. The benefit to both parties is certainty." [15]

1.55. The court found that the agreement between the parties was not a contentious business agreement. Firstly, it held that the agreement was not in writing and further:

"The terms as to charging are not sufficiently fixed. The purpose of a CBA is to fix the fees, or provide a fixing mechanism, so that the parties (and in particular the client) knows where they stand. Under the terms of this document there is still an element of uncertainty. While it is more certain in its charging consequences than the agreement in Chamberlain, it still leaves open the possibility of charging at a higher rate than the specified rates." [16]

---

29 [2007] EWHC 133 (Ch)

1.56. As can be seen, a failure to fix the costs to be charged, or to provide a clear mechanism by which they are to be paid will result in the court finding the retainer is not a business agreement.

1.57. In *Wilson* Mann J stated that whether the retainer states on its face that it is a business agreement is not determinative; the court must look at the terms and consider whether it can properly said to comply with statute.[30]

Challenging costs under a business agreement:

1.58. As a starting point a business agreement, whether in contentious or non-contentious work, has the effect of restricting the client's ability to challenge the fees by way of assessment.

1.59. At s.57(4) relating to non-contentious business agreements the Act states:

> *"the agreement may be sued and recovered on or set aside in the like manner and on the like grounds as an agreement not relating to the remuneration of a solicitor."*

1.60. In relation to contentious business agreements the Act at s.60(1) states:

> *"the costs of a solicitor in any case where a contentious business agreement has been made shall not be subject to assessment"*

1.61. However, as set out below there are important caveats which do mean that in certain circumstances the client can challenge the fees claimed.

1.62. It is important for solicitors to note that they cannot simply bring Part 7 proceedings for payment of fees under a CBA (as thought the matter was a 'normal' debt claim) without the court first considering whether the agreement is enforceable.

---

30 At [14]

1.63. As Kelyn Bacon QC (sitting as a deputy judge of the High Court) put it[31]:

> "...*where the agreement is a contentious business agreement a solicitor cannot sue for his costs by bringing a CPR Part 7 claim. Instead, the court has jurisdiction under an application brought under Part 8 or Part 23, to determine whether the agreement is fair and reasonable. If it is, it may be enforced by the court; if not, then the agreement is to be set aside and the costs are simply to be assessed as if the agreement was not made.*" [26]

Unfair or unreasonable:

1.64. The client can argue that the agreement is unfair or unreasonable. Where this occurs, the court will consider the facts and may set aside the agreement with the effect that the costs will be assessed as if the agreement had not been made (or may reduce the fee charged).

1.65. Even before the enactment of legislation which set out the statutory power of the courts to make such a determination the courts were always cautious to approve such agreements between solicitor and client. In 1907 Fletcher Moulton LJ stated that such agreements[32]:

> "*were ... viewed with great jealousy by the courts, because they were agreements between a man and his legal adviser as to terms of the latter's remuneration, and there was so great an opportunity for the exercise of undue influence, that the courts were very slow to enforce such agreements where they were favourable to the solicitor unless they were satisfied that they were made under circumstances that precluded any suspicion of an improper attempt on the solicitor's part to benefit himself at his client's expense.*"

1.66. For non-contentious business agreements this power is set out within the Act at s.57(5):

---

31 Healys LLP v Partridge and Another [2019] EWHC 2471 (Ch)

32 Clare v Joseph [1907] 2 KB 369

"If on any assessment of costs the agreement is relied on by the solicitor and objected to by the client as unfair or unreasonable, the costs officer may enquire into the facts and certify them to the court, and if from that certificate it appears just to the court that the agreement should be set aside, or the amount payable under it reduced, the court may so order and may give such consequential directions as it thinks fit."

1.67. For contentious business, s.61 of the Act permits the court to set aside an agreement on the same grounds; if the court considers the terms unfair or unreasonable. S.61(2) provides:

"…the court—

(a) if it is of the opinion that the agreement is in all respects fair and reasonable, may enforce it;

(b) if it is of the opinion that the agreement is in any respect unfair or unreasonable, may set it aside and order the costs covered by it to be assessed as if it had never been made;"

1.68. The test for each is the same. In *Bolt Burdon Solicitors v Ai Jaz Tariq*[33] Spencer J cited with approval the words of Lord Esher in *In Re Stuart, ex parte Cathcart*[34]:

"With regard to the fairness of such an agreement, it appears to me that this refers to the mode of obtaining the agreement, and that if a solicitor makes an agreement with a client who fully understands and appreciates that agreement that satisfies the requirement as to fairness. But the agreement must also be reasonable, and in determining whether it is so the matters covered by the expression "fair" cannot be re-introduced. As to this part of the requirements of the statute, I am of opinion that the meaning is that when an agreement is challenged the solicitor must not only satisfy the Court that the agreement was absolutely fair with regard to the way in which it was obtained, but must also satisfy the Court that the terms of that agreement are reasonable. If in the opinion of the Court they are not reasonable having

---

33 [2016] EWHC 811 (QB)

34 [1893] 2 Q.B. 201

regard to the kind of work the solicitor has to do under the agreement, the Court are bound to say that the solicitor, and an officer of the Court, has no right to an unreasonable payment for the work he has done and ought not to have made an agreement for remuneration in such a manner." [148]

1.69. As Spencer J put it in summary:

"Fairness relates principally to the manner in which the agreement came to be made. Reasonableness relates principally to the terms of the agreement." [149]

1.70. Mustil J has made the point that:

"From a practical point of view, the agreement of the client is the strongest evidence that the fee is reasonable".[35]

1.71. Thus, where a client contends that a business agreement is unfair or unreasonable the court will consider each in turn. The *Bolt Burden* case provides an example of the circumstances that the court will consider relevant. In that case the client agreed with the solicitor that the solicitor would be paid by receiving 50% of any compensation recovered, with disbursements in addition. If no compensation was received the solicitor recovered nothing.

1.72. An offer was made and the solicitors became involved. This led to a higher offer being accepted. The fees claimed under the agreement amounted to £498,083.52. In round figures the actual cost of the work undertaken was £50,000.

1.73. The court did not find that the agreement was unfair or unreasonable. In respect of unfairness Spencer J found:

"I am satisfied that the Agreement was not "unfair". Mr Tariq knew exactly what he was agreeing to. He was a very experienced businessman. He was determined that he should pay nothing for Bolt Burdon's services unless and until compensation was received from AIB. He was given an accurate assessment of the prospects of success. Had Mr Bishop told him that the prospects were nearer 20%, rather than

35 Walton v Egan and others - [1982] 3 All ER 849 at 854

"significantly less than 50%", that could only have strengthened Mr Tariq's determination that this was the right Agreement for him." [158]

1.74. As to whether the agreement was unreasonable, the judge stated:

"There is on the face of it an obvious disquiet in permitting solicitors to recover fees of some £400,000 for work which might otherwise have been billed, on the basis of hourly rates, at only some £50,000. However, on proper analysis this ignores the commercial realties which faced the parties when the Agreement was made. In truth the Agreement represented a speculative joint business venture in which the solicitors were taking all the risk and the client was exposed to no risk at all." [164]

1.75. The case of *Vilvarajah v West London Law Ltd*[36] is an example of the court (here the Senior costs judge) finding that a contentious business agreement was unfair and unreasonable. The judge found that the client did not fully understand or appreciate the agreement and as a result it was unfair. Further, the agreement was unreasonable due to the very high hourly rate charged and the peculiar success fee arrangements.

Hourly rates

1.76. Where either a contentious or non-contentious business agreement allows for remuneration by reference to hourly rates and the client is not arguing that the agreement is invalid (or unfair/unreasonable) the client may ask the court to enquire into:

(a) the number of hours worked by the solicitor and

(b) whether that number is excessive[37]

1.77. This power does not extend to the court considering whether the hourly rate itself is fair or reasonable.

---

36 [2017] EWHC B23 (Costs)

37 For non-contentious costs see s.57(7); for contentious costs see s.61(4)

Procedure

1.78. Where a solicitor wishes to enforce an agreement (or a client seeks to challenge it) the procedure depends upon whether the agreement relates to contentious or non-contentious business.

Non-contentious

1.79. S.57(4) of the Act provides that the solicitor may sue on the agreement as though it were a normal debt and not a solicitor and client retainer.

1.80. Save where the agreement allows for payment on the basis of hourly rates (and the client seeks to argue that the number of hours is excessive) the agreement can be relied upon to support the claim and defeat any argument as to the fees.

1.81. If the client seeks to challenge the agreement on the basis that it is not valid or that it is unfair or unreasonable the court will determine that point.

Contentious

1.82. S.61 of the Act provides that there is no cause of action founded upon a business agreement in contentious work. However, on the application of a party to the agreement (or their representative) or a party who is liable to pay the fees the court may:

> "...enforce or set aside the agreement and determine every question as to its validity or effect."[38]

1.83. Following the application the court will then consider whether the agreement is fair and reasonable or, where an hourly rate used, consider whether the hours are excessive.

1.84. The Act at s.61(5) provides that a client who pays the fees may still apply although he will need to show special circumstances. If the application is made more than twelve months after payment the court may still hear the application if it is reasonable to do so.

---

38 S.61(1)

Damages Based Agreements

All change?

1.85. The expansion of DBAs to contentious work in 2013 did not result in solicitors adopting this form of funding in large numbers. The reasons why DBAs are unattractive as a method of funding are set out below.

1.86. As a result, in December 2018 the Ministry of Justice asked Professor Mulheron and Nicholas Bacon QC to carry out an independent review of the Damages-based Agreements Regulations 2013, with a view to re-drafting the Regulations so as to resolve some of the difficulties.

1.87. Following a review, the proposed new rules were published[39]. These have been endorsed by Sir Rupert Jackson.

1.88. Professor Mulheron, co-author of the proposed rules, has said:

> *The DBA redraft moves from an Ontario model to a success fee model. That means the recoverable costs are no longer within the DBA cap; they are outside the DBA cap. So in the event of success, the client must pay three things. Firstly, recoverable costs; secondly, the DBA payment; and thirdly, expenses - which were always outside the DBA cap.*[40]

1.89. There is no doubt that if the rules do allow 'hybrid' DBAs and allow recoverable costs to fall outside the 'cap' DBAs will become a popular and useful method of funding.

1.90. If the proposals are accepted the changes are unlikely to come into effect until at least 2021 (at the earliest).

---

39 https://www.qmul.ac.uk/law/research/impact/dbarp/

40 https://www.lawgazette.co.uk/news/move-towards-workable-dba-regime-through-redrafted-rules/5101826.article

The present DBA rules:

1.91. DBAs are retainers which allow for the payment of the solicitor by the client from the client's damages. In order to recover damages, a claim must be won and so DBAs are another type of contingency fee agreement (along with CFAs).

1.92. DBAs are relatively common in non-contentious work[41] and have never been unlawful. Historically, they were unlawful at common law in contentious work. However, s.58AA of the *Courts and Legal Services Act 1990* (as amended by LASPO[42]) provides that a DBA which complies with that section will not be unenforceable by virtue of the fact that it is a DBA.

1.93. The effect of this is to allow DBAs in contentious work, so long as the provisions of the act are complied with.

The requirements of a DBA

1.94. A DBA must comply with the act and the *Damages Based Agreements Regulations 2013[43]*.

Definition:

1.95. S.58AA(3) of the act defines DBAs thus:

a) a damages-based agreement is an agreement between a person providing advocacy services, litigation services or claims management services and the recipient of those services which provides that—

---

41 Including matters before the Employment Tribunal (due to them historically being considered non-contentious costs), which were required to comply with The Damages Based Agreements Regulations 2010. The regulations apply to DBAs entered into before 1st April 2013. After that date they do not apply, having been revoked.

42 Legal Aid, Sentencing and Punishment of Offenders Act (2012) which came into effect on 1st April 2013

43 It should be noted that the regulations do not apply to any damages-based agreement to which section 57 of the Solicitors Act 1974(5) (non-contentious business agreements between solicitor and client) apply, save in employment matters- reg. (4) and (6).

(i) the recipient is to make a payment to the person providing the services if the recipient obtains a specified financial benefit in connection with the matter in relation to which the services are provided, and

(ii) the amount of that payment is to be determined by reference to the amount of the financial benefit obtained;

1.96. So, to use a simple example, a solicitor could act for a client on the basis that in litigation if damages are recovered they will be paid a percentage of that sum. If no damages are recovered, they recover no fees at all.

Timing:

1.97. A DBA must be entered into on or after 1st April 2013.

Be in writing:

1.98. A DBA must be in writing per s.4(a) of the regulations.

Specify the following:

1.99. Per (3) of the regulations a DBA must specify:

(a) the claim or proceedings or parts of them to which the agreement relates;

(b) the circumstances in which the representative's payment, expenses and costs, or part of them, are payable; and

(c) the reason for setting the amount of the payment at the level agreed, which, in an employment matter, shall include having regard to, where appropriate, whether the claim or proceedings is one of several similar claims or proceedings.

1.100. In relation to employment claims the additional information to be given to the client is as follows (s.5(2) of the regulations):

(a) the circumstances in which the client may seek a review of costs and expenses of the representative and the procedure for doing so;

(b) the dispute resolution service provided by the Advisory, Concili-ation and Arbitration Service (ACAS) in regard to actual and poten-tial claims;

(c) whether other methods of pursuing the claim or financing the pro-ceedings, including—

(i) advice under the Community Legal Service,

(ii) legal expenses insurance,

(iii) pro bono representation, or

(iv) trade union representation, are available, and, if so, how they apply to the client and the claim or proceedings in question; and

(d) the point at which expenses become payable; and

(e) a reasonable estimate of the amount that is likely to be spent upon expenses, inclusive of VAT.

<u>Payment</u>

1.101. The DBA regulations at (4) provide:

"(1) In respect of any claim or proceedings, other than an employ-ment matter, to which these Regulations apply, a damages-based agreement must not require an amount to be paid by the client other than—

(a) the payment, net of—

(i) any costs (including fixed costs under Part 45 of the Civil Proced-ure Rules 1998); and
(ii) where relevant, any sum in respect of disbursements incurred by the representative in respect of counsel's fees,

that have been paid or are payable by another party to the proceed-ings by agreement or order; and

(b) any expenses incurred by the representative, net of any amount which has been paid or is payable by another party to the proceedings by agreement or order."

1.102. The result of this is that the solicitor cannot recover the sums due under the agreement from their client in addition to the costs recoverable between the parties. The amount payable by the client must be net of the costs recovered from the opponent.

1.103. One troubling aspect of the regulation is that the sums payable are net, not just of costs paid by the opponent, but also those 'payable by agreement or order.' Thus, if there is an order for the opponent to pay costs but they are insolvent, or simply refuse to pay, it appears that the solicitor must still account for this sum when billing his client.

Maximum levels of percentages

1.104. The rules do not allow a solicitor and client to agree whatever percentage suits them. Rather, there are maximum percentages that can be applied depending on the type of case to which the DBA applies.

Personal Injury:

1.105. In a claim for personal injury the maximum percentage is 25%.

1.106. The definition of 'a claim for personal injury' is as follows[44]:

"'claim for personal injuries' means proceedings in which there is a claim for damages in respect of personal injuries to the claimant or any other person or in respect of a person's death, and 'personal injuries' includes any disease and any impairment of a person's physical or mental condition;"

1.107. The payment of fees from damages is limited in personal injury cases to[45]:

(i) general damages for pain, suffering and loss of amenity; and

---

44 CPR r.2.3

45 Regulations 4(2)(a)

(ii) damages for pecuniary loss other than future pecuniary loss

net of any sums recoverable by the Compensation Recovery Unit of the Department for Work and Pensions;

1.108. The maximum percentage includes Vat and counsel's fees but not other expenses.

Other Civil claims:

1.109. The maximum percentage of damages that can be recovered under a DBA is 50% including Vat and counsel's fees but not other expenses.

Employment claims:

1.110. The maximum percentage is 35% not including counsel's fee or expenses.

Appeals:

1.111. The above limits do not apply to appeals in civil cases; the solicitor and client may agree any percentage up to 100%.

<u>Indemnity Principle</u>

1.112. One of the most frequent criticisms of the rules relating to DBAs is that the indemnity principle is preserved. This provides that the amount the opponent will pay is limited to the amount that the client is liable to pay his solicitor.

1.113. The CPR at r.44.18 provides that a:

> *"… party may not recover by way of costs more than the total amount payable by that party under the damages-based agreement for legal services provided under that agreement."*

1.114. The effect of the restrictions on the percentage that the solicitor may charge has the effect of making DBAs unattractive (particularly in more modest claims). In reality, unless the claim will be settled quickly, there is little incentive to use a DBA.

1.115. Before considering a DBA the solicitor should carefully calculate:

(a) the amount of damages likely to be recovered

(b) how long the claim will take and when it is likely to settle

(c) what the likely recoverable fees from the opponent would be (where these are fixed costs this should be an easy calculation; if not a costs lawyer or costs draftsman could assist in advising what is likely to be recovered)

(d) what the likely cost of undertaking the work would be (and whether there will be a shortfall between the actual work undertaken and the amount recoverable under the DBA. Solicitors should note that the maximum percentage cannot be exceeded, no matter what is potentially recoverable from the opponent) and work out whether a DBA is suitable. In many circumstances a CFA would be more appropriate, which is why the uptake of DBAs in contentious work has been slow.

1.116. As a rule of thumb, DBAs may be effective where the amount of likely damages can be easily ascertained and the solicitor is confident that the matter is unlikely to drag on to trial. From the solicitor's point of view the ideal DBA case is one where the percentage will be greater than the actual costs incurred. There are types of cases which will likely result in a huge shortfall (uncertain as to quantum, difficult opponent, liability likely to be in dispute, claim likely to reach or go near to trial) and these should never be conducted under a DBA.

1.117. Of course, many claims will be somewhere between the two. Before signing a DBA with the client the solicitor should consider the factors above and then analyse the likely costs recovery when using the various types of retainer. More often than not, a DBA will not be the best option.

Assessment of DBAs

1.118. The CPR at 44.18(1) provides that a costs order will be made in the normal way where the claim is funded by a DBA.

1.119. The rule continues at 44.18(2):

"Where costs are to be assessed in favour of a party who has entered into a damages-based agreement –

(a) the party's recoverable costs will be assessed in accordance with rule 44.3"

1.120. This causes tension and appears to suggest that the costs will be assessed on the standard time multiplied by hourly rate formula. Thus, the costs judge will not stand back and consider whether, as a totality, the sum sought is reasonable and proportionate but rather, assess the costs with the maximum amount acting as a cap.

1.121. This may result in the opponent paying a lower sum than the client is required to pay his solicitor. It also causes potential problems where there is no hourly rate specified within the DBA. How the court will address this issue is not yet clear, although the judge is likely to use an equivalent rate (with reference to the guideline rates and perhaps an uplift) and then assess the hours spent. It is obvious therefore that using a DBA does not absolve the solicitor from properly recording their time; they may need to show the number of hours worked at a between the parties assessment.

Conditional Fee Agreements

1.122. A CFA is another type of contingency fee agreement. They differ from DBAs in the sense that, in a DBA the solicitor agrees to receive a percentage of damages if the claim is won whereas under a CFA the solicitor agrees not to charge the client unless the claim is won and then may apply a success fee in addition to their charges.

1.123. Thus, CFAs are concerned with costs whereas DBAs are concerned with damages. Many of the drawbacks associated with DBAs are not found with CFAs and they remain by far the most popular choice of contingency fee agreement.

1.124. The CFA regime changed dramatically from 1st April 2013 because prior to that date the success fee was recoverable from the opponent if the claim succeeded. Now the client must pay the success fee from damages. As a result, restrictions as to the level of success fee payable (in relation to the damages recovered) have been introduced in some types of claim.

Requirements:

1.125. A CFA must be[46]:

(i) in writing

(ii) not relate to criminal or family litigation
(iii) if the CFA includes a success fee[47]:

(a) it must not be more than 100%

(b) in some types of claim the amount of recoverable costs payable via a success fee may be subject to a maximum limit

(c) the maximum limit must be expressed as a percentage of the descriptions of damages awarded in the proceedings that are specified in the agreement

1.126. As a CFA must be in writing then any variation of the terms must also be written.

Personal Injury:

1.127. This is defined within the Conditional Fee Agreement Regulations 2013 and is the same definition as within the DBA regulations:

---

46 Courts and Legal Services Act 1990 (as amended) s.58

47 Supra.

"'laim for personal injuries' means proceedings in which there is a claim for damages in respect of personal injuries to the claimant or any other person or in respect of a person's death, and 'personal injuries' includes any disease and any impairment of a person's physical or mental condition;"

1.128. As can be seen above, the maximum limit for the success fee relates not to the uplift itself; that can be set at anything up to 100%. Rather, there is a maximum limit in respect of the amount of damages that the client will need to pay in respect of the success fee.

1.129. This limit is 25%. Take for example, a road traffic accident where damages are £3,000. The solicitor's profit costs are £2,000 and the success fee is 50%. At first glance the client will have to pay £1,000 in success fee. They will lose half of their damages.

1.130. However, the cap applies to the effect that the client can only be asked to pay £750 (namely 25% of £3,000).

1.131. The regulations again mirror the DBA rules in respect of what 'damages' are for the purposes of the cap. They are defined as:

"(a) general damages for pain, suffering, and loss of amenity; and

(b) damages for pecuniary loss, other than future pecuniary loss, net of any sums recoverable by the Compensation Recovery Unit of the Department for Work and Pensions."

1.132. The limit only applies to first instance proceedings; on appeals the limit is 100%.

Success Fees in Low Value RTA claims:

1.133. *Herbert v HH Law Ltd*[48] involved a low value RTA which had initially begun within the MOJ portal. The solicitors had set the success fee at 100% on the basis that post LASPO there was no requirement to set the success fee uplift level based on the risk of the individual case. They argued that the 25% cap on the deduction of damages was protec-

---

48 [2019] EWCA Civ 527

tion enough for the client and in any event, by signing the retainer, the client had consented to the 100% uplift.

1.134. The client argued that they had not given "informed consent" to the success fee (because they were not told that it was set without any reference to the risks of losing the case) and that the cap on deductions did not make the 100% uplift reasonable. The district judge at first instance agreed and reduced the success fee to 15%. Soole J at the first appeal upheld the judgment.

1.135. The Court of Appeal also upheld the decision[49].

1.136. It was held that the fixing of success fees in the context of CFAs had traditionally been related to an assessment of the risk of the individual proceedings. Although post LAPSO the Costs Practice Direction relating to assessment of risk had been revoked, the present r.46.9(4):

> "...shows that it was envisaged that a success fee would be related to risk: the reference to the perception of the solicitor or counsel when the conditional fee agreement was entered into or varied closely reflects the language in the former 44PD para. 5 11.7 and 48PD.6 para. 54.5(2)". [50]

1.137. The argument of HH Law that its business model of setting the success fee at 100% in all cases, subject to the 25% cap, was fair and reasonable was rejected because it did not answer the point that a success fee is ordinarily set in relation to litigation risk. The MR stated:

> "I do not consider that either HH's justification for its charging model or the 25% cap answer the point that in this country, in the context of a conditional fee agreement, the amount of a success fee is traditionally related to litigation risk, as reasonably perceived by the solicitor or counsel at the time the agreement was made. Across the broad range of litigation, it would be unusual for it not to be. It continues to be the case in those limited areas, such as publication and privacy proceedings and mesothelioma claims, where success fees are still recoverable from the losing party".[53]

---

49 For discussion of the Court of Appeal's decision on the question of "informed consent" please see Chapter Six.

1.138. Furthermore, the mere fact that many other firms used the same model was insufficient to avoid the need for informed consent, particularly in relation to telling the client that the success fee took no account of any individual risks but was charged as standard in all cases.

1.139. There were huge numbers of CFAs signed in low value RTAs where a 100% success fee has been applied across the board (and taking no account of the actual risks of losing the case in question) prior to the *Herbert* decision. It is highly likely that in all of these cases the success fee will be reduced on assessment to a figure closer to 15% (depending on the risks of the individual cases).

1.140. However, *Herbert* does not say that a solicitor could <u>never</u> charge 100% across the board and in all cases (irrespective of risk) or that a success fee could only ever be calculated based on individualised risk.

1.141. Rather, it requires that a client is given a full and frank explanation as to how the success fee is calculated. Such an explanation must include telling the client that the individual risk is not a factor in setting the success fee (and that this is contrary to the traditional way success fee uplifts have been calculated). In practice, a solicitor would have to be very careful that a lay client properly understood the point and gave informed consent to such a success fee.

Termination of Retainers

1.142. The law relating to termination of the retainer (including consideration of which party may terminate and when) reflects the fact that the relationship between solicitor and client is not equal.

1.143. Put briefly, the law states that a client can terminate a retainer for any reason at any time but restricts the solicitor's ability to terminate to when there is good reason and on reasonable notice.

1.144. The termination of a retainer by either party will not ordinarily (and subject to the terms of the contract) mean that the solicitor loses their right to claim fees. It is only where the termination was:

(a) By the solicitor

(b) Wrongful termination and;

(c) The retainer is an entire contract

that the solicitor will be unable to recover costs.

1.145. This is because if the retainer is an entire contract and the solicitor wrongfully terminates the agreement then per Lord Atkin in *Wild v Simpson*[50] he is not entitled to any costs at all for the work previously undertaken, even on a quantum meruit basis.

The Client

1.146. The client may terminate for any reason and at any time. However, the terms of the retainer may well (and in practice will) impose a liability for the solicitor's costs if the agreement is ended at the client's behest.

The Solicitor

1.147. Under the SRA Code of Conduct solicitors must achieve the following outcome:

> *"when deciding whether to act, or terminate your instructions, you comply with the law and the Code"*[51]

1.148. Under indicative behaviour the Code at 1.26 states:

> *"Acting in the following way(s) may tend to show that you have not achieved these outcomes and therefore not complied with the Principles:*
>
> *• ceasing to act for a client without good reason and without providing reasonable notice".*

1.149. In *Richard Buxton (a firm) v Mills-Owens*[52] Dyson LJ put it thus:

---

50 [1918-19] All ER Rep 682

51 O(1.3)

52 [2010] EWCA Civ 122

"The position at common law is that a solicitor may terminate his retainer before the end on reasonable notice and if he has a 'reasonable ground for refusing to act further for the client'...Where the parties have agreed in what circumstances the solicitor may terminate the retainer, then the matter is governed by their contract. In this case, the parties agreed that the appellants could terminate 'only with good reason'. That reflects the common law position. Unsurprisingly, it also reflects r 12.12 of the Solicitors' Practice Rules." [40]

1.150. The court will imply this term into a retainer. In any event, most retainers as drafted by the solicitor reflect the common law and regulatory position.

1.151. In *Buxton* Dyson LJ made it clear that:

"...solicitors should not lightly be able lawfully to terminate their retainers, leaving their clients with the task of finding fresh solicitors to complete the job." [40]

1.152. Where the retainer is an entire contract the solicitor, absent any contractual terms to the contrary, may only recover fees if he has performed all his duties under the agreement, save where the retainer is terminated with good reason and on reasonable notice.

1.153. Dyson LJ noted in *Buxton* that there was no definition of what is a good reason and that *"whether there is a good reason to terminate is a fact-sensitive question."* [41]

1.154. As a result, an exhaustive list of what would constitute a good reason is not possible, however, it would include:

(i) Where the client asks the solicitor to do something improper or illegal

(ii) Where the is a breakdown in confidence and trust between the solicitor and client due to the client's actions (including where the client loses faith in the ability of the solicitor)[53]

---

53 See for example Minkin v Cawdery Kaye Fireman & Taylor (a firm) (trading as CKFT) - [2012] 3 All ER 1117

(iii) Where the solicitor is unable, despite reasonable attempts, to obtain instructions from their client

(iv) Where the client asks the solicitor to argue a point that is not properly arguable (as in the *Buxton* case)

(v) In contentious business where the solicitor has requested a reasonable payment on account and this is not paid[54]

(vi) Where the client is untruthful, misleads or conceals important facts from his solicitor[55]

1.155. In *Butler v Bankside Commercial Ltd*[56] the CFA allowed the solicitor to terminate the retainer if the client rejected the solcitor's "opinion about making a settlement with your opponent."

1.156. After an offer from the opponent was rejected, the solicitor advised in strong and very detailed terms that a counter-offer of €90,000 plus 50% of costs should be made. The client rejected this advice.

1.157. The solicitor gave the client a deadline within which to accept the advice, failing which the retainer would be terminated. The client did not respond, and the CFA was terminated.

1.158. The client argued that the retainer had been unlawfully terminated because advice about making an offer is not the same as advice about "making a settlement" (which, she argued, was concerned with whether an offer that *had been made* should be accepted; not whether an offer *should be made* by the client).

1.159. The court rejected this argument and found that the termination was reasonable and lawful. At first instance Turner J (in a judgment upheld by the Court of Appeal) stated:

---

54 The Act s.65(2) see also Chapter Three

55 Kris Motor Spares Ltd v Fox Williams LLP [2009] EWHC 2813 (QB) see particularly the judgment at [74] to [85]

56 [2020] EWCA Civ 203

"Where there is no CFA, the client's privilege of ignoring her solicitors' advice, so long as they can continue to act within the boundaries of their professional duties, is preserved intact.

Where, however, there is a CFA under which the solicitors, themselves, face significant economic risks in the event of an adverse result at trial, one would not expect the level of protection which they are afforded against the whims of the unreasonably optimistic client to turn upon the random happenstance of whether or not the other side has made an approach which can be categorised as a contractual offer capable of acceptance..." [21] – [22]

Reasonable notice:

1.160. Even if the retainer were terminated for good reason it would still be for the court to consider whether reasonable notice was given.

1.161. In *Gill v Heer Manak Solicitors*[57] the firm failed to obtain professional indemnity insurance and were given a 90 day period within which to purchase a policy or face closure.

1.162. The solicitors were acting for Mr. Gill in respect of litigation involving worldwide freezing orders obtained by HMRC. They attended a CMC on 20th December with their client but he was not told of any difficulties with the firm. The solicitors did not obtain a policy and on 27th December they wrote to their clients to state that the firm had closed. The client argued that in these circumstances giving no notice of termination of the retainer was not reasonable.

1.163. At first instance Master Simons found for the firm stating that it would have been "commercial suicide" for the firm to tell all of their clients that they were in difficulty.

1.164. This was overturned by Walker J on appeal. The judge said:

"It is essential that such notice as is given is "reasonable". If the notice is not "reasonable" then the firm cannot point to any applicable provision departing from the general principle that remuneration can

---

57 [2018] EWHC 2881 (QB)

only be claimed when all work has been completed, or when there is a natural break. In the absence of reasonable notice, the firm would accordingly be unable to claim for the costs which were sought before the master. It is common ground that when assessing whether notice was "reasonable", the court must apply objective standards." [22] – [23]

1.165. Walker J stated that the result of the termination without notice had a significant prejudicial effect on the client:

"He was left without cover during a period when there might have been significant developments in the litigation, and in any event when a tight timetable had been imposed at the case management hearing on 20 December. Termination of the retainer without notice occurred during the holiday season. I have no doubt that a reasonable observer would have appreciated well before 27 December that termination without notice would risk putting in jeopardy Mr Manjit Gill's ability to comply with that timetable." [33]

1.166. Crucially, the judge found that Master had no basis upon which to make his decision, because the solicitors had failed to put any evidence before the court. As a result, the solicitors were unable to claim any of the fees incurred.

1.167. *Gill* did not find that there could never be any circumstances where giving a client no notice of termination could be reasonable. It does however make clear that it is incumbent upon a solicitor who finds themselves in such a situation to keep a careful record of events leading to the termination and to ensure that the court has sufficient evidence or documentation to enable it to assess whether the decision was reasonable. In the absence of such evidence the court will likely find that the termination was unreasonable and all fees will be lost.

Conditional Fee Agreements

1.168. CFAs are by their very nature entire contracts, because the liability for costs does not crystallise until the claim has ended.

1.169. However, almost every CFA provides for the circumstances in which the solicitor may terminate the agreement. The Law Society

Conditions to their standard model CFA provide that the solicitor can terminate the CFA if the client does not keep to their responsibilities. These set out that the client must:

- *give us instructions that allow us to do our work properly;*
- *not ask us to work in an improper or unreasonable way;*
- *not deliberately mislead us;*
- *co-operate with us;*
- *go to any medical or expert examination or court hearing.*

1.170. If the client does not keep to those responsibilities the solicitor may terminate. They can then decide whether the client must pay their fees (but not success fee) when they ask for them or whether the client must pay the fees (including a success fee) if the claim is won.

Death

1.171. Retainers almost always provide that the death of the client terminates the agreement but that the personal representatives may continue with the action if they subsequently agree.

Incapacity

1.172. The court of appeal in *Blankley v Central Manchester and Manchester Children's University Hospitals NHS Trust*[58] considered whether a retainer was terminated due to incapacity.

1.173. The claimant had capacity when solicitors were retained, but then her capacity to conduct the litigation fluctuated. The issue was whether the CFA terminated automatically by reason of frustration when she subsequently lost capacity, so that it did not govern the continued conduct of the proceedings by a receiver/deputy appointed by the Court of Protection to act on her behalf.

1.174. The court of appeal upheld the decision below that the retainer was not terminated when the client lost capacity. In these circumstances Richard LJ held that the general principles should be qualified to the extent that:

---

58 [2015] EWCA Civ 18

"(i) the solicitor retains authority to act so long as he is unaware of the incapacity and (ii) he retains authority to take necessary steps in consequence of the incapacity, including an application to the court for the appointment of a deputy and/or litigation friend, when he does become aware of it. It might also be preferable to talk in terms of "suspension" rather than "termination" of authority, on the basis that the solicitor's authority is restored if the client regains capacity or a litigation friend is appointed to continue the litigation on the client's behalf." [36]

1.175. The judge concluded:

"The fact that supervening incapacity prevented the claimant from giving instructions personally did not render the contract of retainer impossible of performance; it simply gave rise to a short period of delay pending appointment of a receiver/deputy who could continue the conduct of the proceedings on the claimant's behalf and give instructions to the solicitors for that purpose." [38]

CHAPTER TWO
ESTIMATES

Introduction

2.1. A client who instructs a solicitor in a contentious matter will always want to know two things at the outset; what the merits are and what the cost will be. In non-contentious matters the client will similarly be concerned as to the costs of the work.

2.2. The simplest way to ensure that both solicitor and client know what the cost will be is for the client to be given a fixed quote at the outset. That quote will not change and will provide certainty for both parties.

2.3. Fixed fees are eminently suitable for some types of work (particularly non-contentious legal work such as property transfers) where the potential amount of work the solicitor will do can be easily ascertained at the outset. However, in many other types of legal work a fixed quotation is a recipe for under payment. Litigation is an obvious example. In litigation the amount of work the solicitor must undertake can be increased by factors outside of their control- a problematic opponent for example.

2.4. The SRA Code of Conduct for Solicitors 2018 requires that a solicitor should (a) clearly explain their fees and (b) if and when they are likely to change. The Code at 8.7 states that solicitors must:

> *"…ensure that clients receive the best possible information about how their matter will be priced and, both at the time of engagement and when appropriate as their matter progresses, about the likely overall cost of the matter and any costs incurred."*

2.5. Where a fixed price is quoted and accepted there is little potential for dispute; the client will pay that amount whatever the work undertaken (and the solicitor will not be able to charge more without the consent of the client).

2.6. Where a fixed price is not agreed the solicitor should provide an estimate of the cost of the work at the outset. As shall be seen estimates have the potential to cause issues for the solicitor where they prove inadequate and where the client has relied upon them.

2.7. The remainder of this chapter will focus on estimates.

The Golden Rules

2.8. Estimates become problematic where there are inadequate, not properly explained and where the solicitor does not regularly keep them updated.

2.9. Following these rules should keep disputes to a minimum:

(i) Ensure the first estimate is accurate

2.10. The understandable reluctance of a solicitor to provide an estimate that has the potential to scare off a client should not dissuade them from providing a sensible estimate at the outset.

2.11. The fee earner providing the estimate should be experienced enough to be able to properly estimate the likely cost of the work. The estimate should not be given on a 'best case scenario' but rather be a realistic band of figures which takes into account a smooth-running case at one end and a case where far more work will be needed at the other.

2.12. If the fee earner is not sufficiently experienced to properly estimate what the cost will be then they should discuss the issue with a supervisor or partner in the firm.

2.13. Taking sufficient time to provide an accurate initial estimate will avoid many potential problems. It is striking how many solicitors provide inadequate estimates at the outset. As will be seen, in some circumstances an inadequate initial estimate may not be cured by revisions at a later date.

2.14. Thought should be given as to whether it would be beneficial to provide estimates in stages rather than for the entire action. For example, an estimate could be given for bringing the matter to proceedings. Thereafter, to bring the matter to a CMC and then a pre-trial review. Finally, a figure can be given to take the case all the way to trial. Breaking the estimates down into these phases can mean that the figures are far more accurate. Of course, a client will likely still want to have an idea of the overall cost but the staged approach allows:

(a) more accurate estimates

(b) natural points where an estimate can be discussed and revised if the claim is taking longer or becoming more complicated. This can mean the next stage estimate and the overall figure can be revised in consultation with the client.

(ii) Ensure the estimate is properly worded.

2.15. When providing the initial estimate it is essential to set out in clear language that the figures quoted are estimates only, are subject to change and are not a fixed quote.

2.16. The following wording is suggested:

> *"It is important that you understand the likely level or amount of our fees for undertaking this work.*
>
> *At this stage it is impossible to set out a precise figure for the cost because there are a number of factors which could increase the amount of work we are required to do. In our experience we estimate that the cost of the work will be between £X and £Y.*
>
> *This is not a fixed price quote and is an estimate only. The amount you are required to pay us may be higher than this depending on what occurs during the period we are instructed. We will revise the estimate if at any time the likely cost will rise or fall. If that happens we will discuss with you the reasons for the revision before the estimate is altered.*
>
> *We will write to you with an updated estimate every 3 months during the period of our instructions. If you are concerned as to the level of costs or wish to make a decision in respect of the claim which re-*

quires you to have an up to date estimate of costs you may ask us for such an up to date figure at any time."

(iii) Keep the estimate updated

2.17. It is understandable that sometimes initial estimates prove inaccurate but there is no excuse for allowing such an estimate to remain untouched as the work progresses.

2.18. The solution is simple; diarise the matter for review at regular periods and check whether the last estimate is still accurate. If not, revise it and tell the client. It is far better to have a discussion of the likely costs (and why they may change) during the retainer than have a dispute with a disgruntled client once it is at an end.

2.19. If an estimate is to be significantly revised then there should be a justification for this. What has changed since the original estimate? Why could this change not be foreseen at the outset? These are the questions that a court will ask if the estimate proves to be an issue at a later assessment.

Giving No Estimate

2.20. It might be thought that giving no estimate at all would place the solicitor in a better position than providing an estimate which could turn out to be inadequate.

2.21. In *Garbutt v Edwards*[1] (a between the parties assessment) it had been argued that a failure to give an estimate rendered the retainer unlawful. That was rejected by the court of appeal who held that where no estimate is given this is merely a factor for the costs judge to take into account.

2.22. There is no obvious sanction within the rules, Act or case law for a solicitor who fails to give an estimate. However, two points should be noted; firstly, that a failure to give an estimate is a clear breach of the code of conduct and secondly, a client could argue that had a reasonable estimate been given they would possibly have approached the matter differently (and as a result this should be taken into account when

1 [2005] EWCA Civ 1206

the costs judge assesses what it would be reasonable for the client to pay).

2.23. In *Newman v Gordon Dadds LLP*[2] the costs judge set out the principles thus:

> *"From those authorities one can distil the following principles. If, on the assessment of costs between a solicitor and a client, it is found (a) that the solicitor has never provided the client with an estimate of the costs that the client was likely to pay and (b) that if a proper estimate had been given, the client would have paid less than the solicitor is claiming, it may be appropriate to limit the amount payable by the client to the solicitor to an amount that it is reasonable, in all the circumstances, to expect the client to pay. That may be less than would otherwise be payable for work reasonably done by the solicitor at a reasonable rate."* [69]

2.24. It would be most unadvisable to risk sanction by the SRA or the costs judge for failing to provide an estimate.

When Can a Solicitor Be Held to the Estimate?

2.25. Unless an estimate is a considered a fixed price quote the solicitor will never be held to an estimate. Rather, when considering what it is reasonable for the client to pay, the estimate will be taken into account where:

(a) the figures provided prove inadequate and the actual costs exceed the amounts quoted.

(b) where the estimate has not been properly explained (if the client can argue that it was a fixed quote then it could act as a cap on the recoverable fees).

(c) where there is no adequate explanation for the overspend.

(d) if the client can show reliance upon the estimate then the solicitor may be held to the sum (although the estimate will never operate as a cap).

---

2 [2020] EWHC B23 (Costs)

2.26. The leading case on solicitor and client estimates is *Mastercigars Direct Ltd v Withers LLP*[3]. Here, the solicitors exceeded their estimate and at first instance were restricted to that amount. They appealed that decision to the High Court where Morgan J gave judgment on the general principles. The matter was remitted back to the costs judge to consider reliance and this decision was appealed back to Morgan J[4]. Finally, the Court of Appeal refused permission to appeal in a written judgment[5].

2.27. Morgan J set out the legal principle in the first *Mastercigars* judgment thus:

> "In a case where a solicitor does give his client an estimate but the costs subsequently claimed exceed the estimate, it will not follow in every case that the solicitor will be restricted to recovering the sum in the estimate". [92]

2.28. Rather, the proper position was set out as follows:

> "The estimate is a useful yardstick by which the reasonableness of the costs may be measured. If there is a modest difference between the estimate and the final bill, because an estimate is not a fixed price for the work, one may be very little surprised by the modest difference. The greater the difference, the more it calls for an explanation. If there is a satisfactory explanation for the difference then the estimate may cease to be useful as a yardstick with which to measure reasonableness. Conversely, if there is no satisfactory explanation the estimate may remain a very useful yardstick with which to measure reasonableness." [99]

2.29. In other words, when the costs judge is assessing the solicitor's bill he may use the estimate as 'a useful yardstick' which assists in informing him as to the reasonable level of costs. That does not mean that the solicitor is limited to the estimate amount but if he wishes to recover costs in excess of an estimate (particularly where the difference is not modest) then the court will expect an explanation as to the difference.

---

3   [2007] EWHC 2733 (Ch)

4   [2009] EWHC 1295 (Ch)

5   [2009] EWCA Civ 1526

2.30. Per Morgan J the ultimate question is what in all the circumstances is it reasonable for the client to pay:

"...in some cases, the solicitors' estimate will be a useful yardstick with which to measure the reasonableness of the final bill and in other cases the amount of the estimate will be a factor in considering what sum it is reasonable to expect the client to pay". [103]

Reliance Upon an Estimate

2.31. The second *Mastercigars* judgment was concerned with the question of the courts approach where a client can show that they relied upon the estimate. Morgan J at [54] set out the steps the court should take when considering this issue (said to be *"put forward as practical guidance rather than as a legal imperative"*) thus [6]:

"In my judgment, the legal process involved in a case where a client contends that its reliance on an estimate should be taken into account in determining the figure which it is reasonable for the client to pay is as follows..

- *The court should determine whether the client did rely on the estimate.*

- *The court should determine how the client relied on the estimate...without conducting an elaborate and detailed investigation.*

- *The court should decide whether the costs claimed should be reduced by reason of its findings as to reliance and, if so, in what way and by how much.*

- *Whether there should be a reduction, and if so to what extent, is a matter of judgment. Specific deductions can be made from the costs otherwise recoverable to reflect the impact which an erroneous and uncorrected estimate had on the conduct of the client.*

---

6   These steps have been separated for ease of reading. In the original judgment they are all included within one paragraph with no breaks.

- *Such an approach requires the court to form an assessment of the impact of the estimate on the conduct of the client.*

- *The court should consider the deductions which are needed in order to do justice between the parties.*

- *It is not the proper function of the court to punish the solicitor for providing a wrong estimate or for failing to keep it up to date as events unfolded."* [54]

2.32. In respect of the burden upon the client, the judge held:

"...the client did not have to go so far as to show the ingredients of an estoppel against the solicitor. One part of my reasoning was that it would often be difficult for a client to show that "he would have" acted differently but the client may be able to show "it is possible he might have approached the litigation differently" if he had been given a more accurate estimate. Thus, my formulation of what is required does not go so far as to require the client to prove on the balance of probabilities that he would have acted differently". [47]

2.33. As can be seen, all that is required is that the client can show that it is <u>possible</u> that he might have approached the litigation differently had an accurate estimate been provided.

<u>A margin above the estimate</u>

2.34. In the second *Mastercigars* judgment Morgan J noted[7] that costs judges had, since *Wong v Vizards (A Firm)*[8] adopted a margin approach (often said to be 15% or 20%) to determining the reasonable costs payable by the client. Put simply, they would limit the solicitor to the estimate and then add on a percentage margin to allow for the fact that the estimate was not a fixed quote.

2.35. However, the court in *Wong* had never suggested that a margin over and above the estimate should be allowed as a general practice. In fact what Toulson J did in that case was to work out what he considered

7 [56]: "...the margin approach is very much favoured by Costs Judges."

8 [1997] 2 Cost LR 46

would be the reasonable costs taking into account the estimate (which happened to be a figure of the estimate plus 15%). Despite this, first instance decisions in cases where estimates had been exceeded began to use the 'estimate plus 15%' rule of thumb appeared and many in the profession took this to be a rule of general application. It was never so.

2.36. Morgan J in the first *Mastercigars* judgment made it very clear that the idea of the 'estimate plus a % margin' was erroneous [104-105]. In the second judgment he made this clear, stating:

> "...the adoption of a margin approach greatly simplifies the steps which a Costs Judge needs to take when carrying out a detailed assessment of a bill, which has been preceded by a lower estimate... it is obvious, at least to me, that the adoption of a margin approach as the conventional approach in the majority of cases pays scant, if any, attention to the legal process which I attempted to describe in my earlier judgment and have now restated in paragraph 54 above." [57]

2.37. That is not to say that that a court, when properly taking the steps required and asking itself what in all the circumstances is it reasonable for the client to pay, can never express itself by reference to a margin. However, the judge must consider the issue fully and properly and cannot short cut the process by simply allowing an estimate plus 15 or 20%.[9]

2.38. Despite the law being clarified for many years it is still common to see clients arguing that costs should be restricted to an estimate plus a margin. That is not the correct approach.

Initial inadequate estimate revised

2.39. If a solicitor provides an estimate at the outset which is inadequate then revising that estimate will not necessarily mean the court disregards the original.

2.40. The case of *Reynolds v Stone Rowe Brewer*[10] provides a salutary warning to solicitors when setting estimates at the outset.

---

9 See [57] of the Second Mastercigars judgment

10 [2008] EWHC 497 (QB)

2.41. The claimant in this case instructed solicitors in relation to a dispute with her builder. The builder issued proceedings and she counter claimed, eventually recovering damages of £55,380.

2.42. The claimant's solicitors advised at the outset that *"If the matter did proceed through to a trial, it is more than likely that your costs would be in the region of £10,000 to £18,000 plus VAT, and this is only of course an estimate which could be increased depending on how strenuously the matter is defended."*

2.43. Throughout the claim the solicitors increased this estimate numerous times. By the final revised estimate their bills totalled £59,400.35 and their estimate of their costs to trial was £55,000 plus vat.

2.44. In fact, by the end of the matter the claimant's total costs liability (including the fees of the second firm instructed to take over the matter) was £90,000.

2.45. At the first hearing before the costs judge the solicitors sought to justify why the original estimate was so inadequate. The costs judge found that this did not explain the difference and allowed the solicitor the sum of £18,000 plus Vat (the top end of the original estimate) with a margin of 15% in addition. The solicitors appealed.

2.46. Tugendhat J also held that the explanations for the overspend did not justify the inadequate estimate:

> *"While I accept that by the time the estimate of £60,000 was given there had been some unusual developments in the form of the applications which the Claimant instructed the solicitors to oppose, contrary to their advice, these cannot explain the bulk of the difference between the ultimate claim by the solicitors and their earlier estimates".* [68]

2.47. The judge commented that:

> *"This case has been a disastrous experience for the Claimant, and little better for the solicitors. The Claimant embarked on litigation*

which she could not by any means afford, on the understanding, conveyed by the solicitors, that she could just afford it." [69]

2.48. He went on to say:

"…it is by no means uncommon for a Claimant who recovers, as this Claimant did, a judgment for some £55,380.80, to incur costs in excess of that amount in so doing. In this case it was never the intention of either the Claimant or the solicitor that such a state of affairs should come about. It came about because the estimates in 2005, including the November 2005 estimate, were unreasonably low." [69]

2.49. And further that:

"In my judgment the Costs Judge was fully entitled to come to the view that, if the estimates given at the start of the case had been such as are required by the applicable rules, then the Claimant would not have acted as she did. She would clearly not have been able to afford to do so, and I think it unlikely she would have embarked on the course she did embark on." [70]

2.50. The conclusion of the judge was:

"I assume that the solicitors have spent a reasonable time on reasonable items of work, and that the charging rate is reasonable. But I find that the resulting figure exceeds what it is reasonable in all the circumstances to expect the client to pay. The figure that the Costs Judge certified is a figure that it is reasonable to expect the Claimant to pay in this case." [71]

2.51. As a result, the solicitors recovered only the costs contained within the original estimate plus a margin. Had the solicitors provided a reasonable and realistic estimate at the outset they could have avoided all of the problems that followed. Of course, had they done so the claimant may never have taken on the claim in the first place.

2.52. This case and others[11] demonstrate that simply revising an inadequate estimate given at the outset may not mean the court will only take into account the later revisions (particularly if the client can show

---

11 See for example Harrison v Eversheds [2017] EWHC 2594 (QB)

reliance). It is imperative that solicitors endeavour to get the estimate right at the start of the retainer.

Budgets and Estimates

2.53. The rules relating to costs budgets apply to certain types of cases only and are concerned with the reasonable and proportionate sums payable between the parties.[12]

2.54. Since costs budgets are set with proportionality in mind and on the basis of what may reasonably be recoverable between the parties (rather than on a solicitor and own client basis) it cannot be said that a budget represents the amount that a client is liable or even likely to pay to his *own* solicitors; rather it sets out the amount likely to be paid by the opponent if the claim succeeds.

2.55. However, in respect of estimated costs, a budget approved by the court does show the sums recoverable between the parties (and will not be departed from unless the party can show good reason). It is therefore an extremely useful document to provide to a client.

2.56. Good practice (and the code of conduct) dictates that a solicitor should ensure that the client sees the approved budget. If costs are incurred outside the parameters of that budget then it is likely that the court will find that they fall within CPR r.46(c) and will be presumed to be unreasonably incurred.[13]

2.57. Further, the provisions at s.74(c) of the Act and CPR r.46.9(2) mean that in contentious county court cases the solicitor will be limited to the costs recoverable between the parties unless there is agreement to the contrary.[14] In these circumstances the budget is clearly an important document within the solicitor client context.

2.58. As a result, where a costs budget is approved or agreed, the solicitor should send this to the client and explain that it represents the costs that will be recovered between the parties if the case is won (but

---

12 The rules are set out at CPR Part 3 II (r.3.12 -3.18) and PD 3E

13 See Chapter Six

14 See Chapter One

do not include the costs that the client will be liable to pay on a solicitor client basis). If costs are incurred outside the budget (and the budget is not revised) then the client must be told that these are unlikely to be recovered at the end of the claim.

2.59. There is much to commend the practice of a costs lawyer preparing a solicitor and client budget (at the same time as the between the parties budget is approved) and serving this on the client. This will ensure that the client has a good idea of the overall cost to them and the likely amount that the opponent will pay if the claim is successful.

CHAPTER THREE
STATUTE BILLS

Introduction

3.1. Before a solicitor may begin an action to recover costs or a client can request the court assess the fees charged two things must occur:

(i) the solicitor must prepare a statute bill.

(ii) that bill must be delivered to the client.

3.2. It should be obvious what a solicitor's bill is; it is the notice of charges that is sent to the client for payment. However, as this chapter shows, the issue is complex and the question of when a document is a statute bill frequently arises during disputes between solicitors and their clients.

3.3. The reason for this is that bills are either 'statute bills' (that is, a bill that complies with the requirements of s.69 of the Act and the case law which has clarified the circumstances when a bill is compliant) or non-statute bills which do not comply with the Act or case law.

3.4. The reason for the importance of the status of an invoice is that if the invoice is a statute bill and the bill has been delivered the solicitor can bring an action to recover his costs.

3.5. If the invoice is not a statute bill then it is simply a request for a payment on account. No action can be taken to recover the costs contained within the invoice.

3.6. In those circumstances, before any action can be taken by either the solicitor or the client, there must be a statute bill prepared and delivered.

3.7. It is worth noting that in the ordinary course of events if there is no statute bill delivered (or the client challenges the status of a bill -arguing that it is not a statute bill- and is successful) there cannot be an assessment. The court can only assess a statute bill under the Act. Two authorities make the point clear:

(a) In *Re: Baylis[1]* the court of appeal confirmed that the retention by a solicitor of payment of costs is not payment of the bill and does not affect the client's right to an assessment. In that case the solicitor argued that his accounts had been settled and the bills were paid. That was not correct. Per Lindley LJ:

> "We cannot hold that the accounts were settled and the bills paid, as no bills had ever been delivered."

Chitty J, whose decision below was upheld, made the point clearly:

> "It cannot be questioned on the facts that no bill of costs was ever delivered. By "bill of costs" I mean what the Solicitors Act, 1843, says, namely, a bill of fees, charges, and disbursements. I entirely dissent from the argument that there are two kinds of solicitors' bills. There is only one, as is shewn by numerous authorities."

(b) In *Vlamaki v Sookias & Sookias[2]* the client sought an assessment of invoices rendered. She then argued successfully that invoices sent were merely request for payments on account and not statute bills. However, she went on to argue that a letter notifying her that no further charges were to be levied was the final bill in a series and meant all could be assessed. Walker J found against her. The effect of the first decision was that there were no bills to assess and the court found that the commencement of assessment proceedings had been premature.

3.8. There are exceptional circumstances where a bill which is not technically a statute bill will be assessed. An example is the 'bill' in *Ex p d'Aragon[3]*:

(i) There the client sought a statute bill and one was delivered although it was unsigned. The solicitors had not signed it as a cynical ruse to enable them to replace it with a fresh bill if the client challenged the fees.

---

1   [1895 B. 172.] - [1896] 2 Ch. 107

2   [2015] EWHC (QB) 3334

3   3 TLR 815

(ii) The client sought an assessment of the bill and this was denied by the Master at first instance and a Judge in chambers because the bill was not a statute bill. The Divisional Court found that the bill should be assessed because the solicitor *"could not, so to speak, 'try it on' and deliver bills to his client not singed to escape taxation."*

(iii) The Court of Appeal agreed. The bill had been delivered as such pursuant to a request from the client and the solicitor could not rely upon their breach of the Act to their advantage.[4]

3.9. It should be noted that *Ex p d'Aragon* does not run against the authority that only a statute bill can be assessed. Rather, it is support for the argument that where a solicitor delivers a statute bill he cannot disregard it due to a technical deficiency if the client wishes to have it assessed (particularly if the court find that the technical deficiency was a deliberate act).

3.10. Where there is a dispute about the statute of bills the client should seek either a determination of their status as a preliminary issue or seek an order for delivery up (see below). If the solicitor asserts that the invoice is a statute bill then this question can be decided by the court at the preliminary issue hearing.

Bills on Account[5]

3.11. If an invoice sent to a client is not a statute bill then it is simply a request for a payment on account. As can be seen, such an invoice may not be used as the basis for a claim to recover the sums sought.

3.12. It follows that the formalities required of a statute bill set out below do not apply to such an invoice. So long as the request for payment is clear, legible and can be understood by the client it will be a valid request.

---

4 See in contrast Parvez v Mooney Everett at 3.38 below where the court found against a client who made a similar argument for the reason that in that case the solicitor had never intended to deliver the bill.

5 Often called 'non-statute bills' or 'requests for payments on account' for obvious reasons

3.13. The advantage of seeking a payment on account are obvious in terms of cash flow but there are other reasons why a solicitor may make such a request. If the client does not pay a reasonable sum sought within a reasonable time then in contentious business the solicitor may use this as a good reason to terminate the retainer on reasonable notice. This is set out in s.65(2) of the Act:

> *"If a solicitor who has been retained by a client to conduct contentious business requests the client to make a payment of a sum of money, being a reasonable sum on account of the costs incurred or to be incurred in the conduct of that business and the client refuses or fails within a reasonable time to make that payment, the refusal or failure shall be deemed to be a good cause whereby the solicitor may, upon giving reasonable notice to the client, withdraw from the retainer".*

3.14. The question of what sum and time scale was reasonable will be fact specific.

3.15. While the disadvantages of rendering bills on account is that they cannot be relied upon to begin an action for recovery of the fees (and do not begin the time running for assessment under the Act) they have the advantage of not being final. That is to say, they are subject to a final statute bill which can be for a greater sum.

Delivery Up

3.16. Where no statute bill exists and the client wishes to have the charges assessed, he may make an application for delivery up of a statute bill under s.69 of the Act.

3.17. Such an application is made using the Part 8 procedure. Prior to issuing the claim the client should make a formal request for delivery and allow the solicitor adequate time to prepare their statute bill. In the proceedings the remedy sought will be:

> *"The claimant seeks delivery up of a statute bill pursuant to s.68 Solicitors Act 1974 in respect of the work undertaken by X Solicitors from X to X under the retainer dated X."*

3.18. If the client has informally sought a statute bill and the solicitor has delayed unreasonably it is often worth seeking an Unless Order at the same time as the delivery up order is made. For example, the order sought at the hearing of the application would be:

> *"Unless by 18th September 2018 X Solicitors do deliver to Mr. X a final statute bill in respect of the work undertaken between X and X under the retainer dated X then all of the costs to which they would otherwise be entitled to will be disallowed."*

3.19. The courts will ordinarily provide a generous time period for the preparation and delivery of the bill, particularly in high value matters or where the costs cover a long period of time.

3.20. The High Court has the power to order delivery up of a bill even where the work undertaken was not brought in that court6. Thus, the SCCO will ordinarily be the venue of choice for such applications.

3.21. However, the county and family court each have the same jurisdiction where:

(i) the bill relates wholly or partly to contentious business and

(ii) the claim was brought in the county or family court respectively.[7]

When Is a Bill Required?

3.22. The Solicitors Account Rules[8] set out when a bill must be sent. In short, a solicitor must deliver a bill before transferring money for payment of fees from client account to office account.

3.23. It also requires that once a bill is sent, the fees must be transferred out of client account into the office account with 14 days.

3.24. The rules provide:

---

6 The Act s.68(1)

7 The Act s.68(2)

8 https://www.sra.org.uk/solicitors/handbook/accountsrules/content.page

"17.2 If you properly require payment of your fees from money held for a client or trust in a client account, you must first give or send a bill of costs, or other written notification of the costs incurred, to the client or the paying party.

17.3 Once you have complied with rule 17.2 above, the money earmarked for costs becomes office money and must be transferred out of the client account within 14 days."

3.25. A solicitor must keep records of the bills or written notification of costs delivered to clients. The Accounts Rules state:

"29.15 You must keep readily accessible a central record or file of copies of:

(a) all bills given or sent by you (other than those relating entirely to activities not regulated by the SRA); and

(b) all other written notifications of costs given or sent by you (other than those relating entirely to activities not regulated by the SRA)."

3.26. The Guidance Note to this rule provides:

"(x): The rules do not require a bill of costs for an agreed fee, although your VAT position may mean that in practice a bill is needed. If there is no bill, the written evidence of the agreement must be filed as a written notification of costs under rule 29.15(b)."

3.27. Read as a whole the rules do suggest that a written notification of costs, rather than a bill, is suitable where the fees are a fixed sum agreed between the solicitor and client. If the costs are not a fixed agreed sum then the written notification would likely need to contain a sufficient level of detail to allow inspection of the fees claimed.

3.28. Of course, even if a written notification of costs is sent to the client for the purposes of transferring the sums from client to office, then a statute bill would still need to be delivered before the solicitor could sue for his fees or the costs could be assessed. In those circumstances there is little incentive for a solicitor to deliver anything other than a statute bill (save where the fees are an agreed fixed sum).

The Formalities Under the Act[9]

3.29. Somewhat surprisingly, the Act itself does not contain a great deal of formalities for statute bills. The provisions are set out in s.69 and state that in order to be a statute bill the document must be:

(i) Signed in accordance with sub-section 2(a).

(ii) Delivered in accordance with sub-section 2(c).

Signature

3.30. Sub-section 2(a) states:

> *"A bill is signed in accordance with this subsection if it is—*
> *(a) signed by the solicitor or on his behalf by an employee of the solicitor authorised by him to sign, or*
>
> *(b) enclosed in, or accompanied by, a letter which is signed as mentioned in paragraph (a) and refers to the bill."*

3.31. Note that the Partner of the firm or even a solicitor does not need to sign the bill. An unqualified employee may sign the bill, so long as he is authorised to do so.

3.32. As can be seen, the bill itself may be unsigned, so long as the covering letter is signed <u>and</u> refers to the bill itself.

3.33. The signature can be an electronic signature.[10]

3.34. The signature may be in the form of the firm name[11] and may even be an abbreviation of the firm name[12].

---

9 The Act was amended from March 2008 and the previous version should be consulted in relation to bills before this time.

10 S.69 (2)(b)

11 Goodman v J Eban Ltd [1954] 1 QB 550

12 Bartletts de Reya v Byrne [1983] Lexis Citation 1722- the firm's name was 'Bartlett & Gluckstein, Crawley & de Reya' the bill was signed 'Bartletts' but also contained the full firm name. This was held to be sufficient by Fox LJ although he warned:

<u>Delivery</u>

3.35. In terms of delivery, sub section 2(c) states:

> *"A bill is delivered in accordance with this subsection if—*
>
> *(a) it is delivered to the party to be charged with the bill personally,*
>
> *(b) it is delivered to that party by being sent to him by post to, or left for him at, his place of business, dwelling-house or last known place of abode,*
>
> *or*
>
> *(c) it is delivered to that party—*
>
> *(i) by means of an electronic communications network, or*
>
> *(ii) by other means but in a form that nevertheless requires the use of apparatus by the recipient to render it intelligible, and that party has indicated to the person making the delivery his willingness to accept delivery of a bill sent in the form and manner used.*
>
> *(2D) An indication to any person for the purposes of subsection (2C) (c)—*
>
> *(a) must state the address to be used and must be accompanied by such other information as that person requires for the making of the delivery;*
>
> *(b) may be modified or withdrawn at any time by a notice given to that person."*

3.36. These provisions are clear and easily understood. The bill may be emailed if the client indicates that they would accept delivery in this way and provide an email address to use (only delivery to that particular

"the form of signature on solicitors bills does seem to have given trouble now and again down the years and it would be a sensible course if solicitors wish to put matters beyond question, to sign in the name of the firm in full". In the present climate, with solicitors' firm's official names tending to be very short abbreviations it is thought that this issue would arise very infrequently.

email address will suffice). Further, the bill may be faxed (2(c)(ii) above) again only if the client has indicated that this is an accepted means of delivery.

3.37. Solicitors should note that the client can withdraw an indication to accept delivery by electronic means at any time. It is worth checking that no such withdrawal of consent has been provided before electronically delivering the bill.

3.38. Soole J has found that a document which is capable of being a statute bill cannot be assessed if it is not delivered by the solicitor; even where the 'bill' comes into the possession of the client and the client wishes to elect to accept delivery:

> "It must follow that it is only the solicitor who can determine the content and terms of what is his demand or claim for payment. Neither the client nor the court can make that determination on his behalf... It is for the solicitor to provide 'a bill' of his costs; and for the process of assessment to deal with any challenge thereto."[13]

3.39. The bill should be delivered to the client unless they have indicated that it can be delivered to new solicitors acting on their behalf or the court has otherwise ordered[14].

3.40. Finally, even without formal delivery of a statute bill a solicitor may set off costs against damages.[15]

Disbursements

3.41. If there are disbursements which have not yet been paid they should be included within the bill as delivered. Per s.67 of the Act they must be described in the bill as not paid.

3.42. It is imperative that they are paid before the assessment is completed. S.67(b) provides that if the bill is assessed the court will not al-

---

13 Parvez v Mooney Everett Solicitors [2018] EWHC 62 (QB) at [57] and [58].

14 Vincent v Slaymaker (1810) 104 ER 146

15 Brown v Tibbits (1862) 11 C.B. N.S. 855

low recovery of the fees unless they are paid before the assessment is completed.

3.43. Where a solicitor finds themselves in this position the only obvious remedies are to either pay the disbursements before the assessment concludes or to seek an adjournment (inevitably at their own expense).

ATE premiums

3.44. In *Herbert v HH Law*[16], the court of appeal held that an ATE premium[17] is not a solicitor's disbursement, but rather, is a client disbursement:

> "It is a premium on a policy of insurance under which the client is the insured, pursuant to a contract of insurance made between the insurer and the client, in order to provide the client with funds to discharge costs which are not recovered from the opposing party and the client is liable to pay, whether those are costs of the other party or of the client's own solicitors." [68].

3.45. As a result, an ATE premium should not be included within the statute bill[18] and cannot be objected to within a Solicitors Act assessment.[19]

Rebuttable Presumption that a Bill Complying with the Act is a Statute Bill

3.46. It is clear therefore that where a bill does not comply with the Act it is not a statute bill. However, even compliance with the Act does not automatically mean a bill has this status. S.69 (2)(E) provides that:

> "Where a bill is proved to have been delivered in compliance with the requirements of subsections (2A) and (2C), it is not necessary in the first instance for the solicitor to prove the contents of the bill and it is

16 [2019] EWCA Civ 527

17 Namely, the cost of purchasing a policy of insurance in order to insure against having to pay the client's opponent's costs.

18 But should be included within the cash account.

19 See the judgment at [71]

to be presumed, until the contrary is shown, to be a bill bona fide complying with this Act".

3.47. Thus, if a bill complies with the Act it will be presumed to be a statute bill until and unless the client shows otherwise. This is because a body of case law has built up which demands further requirements from a statute bill and a client who is served with a bill complying with the strict terms of the Act may still be able to show that the bill does not have this status.[20]

Requirements of a Statue Bill: Case Law

3.48. As can be seen, compliance with the Act is not the end of the matter. The bill must also comply with the various principles set out within the authorities.

3.49. In summary, in order to be a statute bill the invoice must:

(i) contain a sufficient narrative

(ii) be a reasonably complete account of the fees rendered under the retainer

(iii) allow the client to consider whether to have the fees assessed

(iv) allow the court to assess the bill

(v) be a demand or request for payment

3.50. It is worth repeating that once the terms of the Act are complied with, the burden is on the <u>client</u> to show that the bill is not a valid statute bill.

---

20 As Ward LJ remarked in Ralph Hume Garry (a firm) v Gwillim - [2002] EWCA Civ 1500 "There is no other hint or help in the Act to determine what is or is not bona fide compliance with the Act. To discover the answer one may have to trawl through statute and case law stretching back over 273 years." [15]

Sufficient Narrative

3.51. A narrative is the description of the work undertaken and does not refer to the breakdown of the items. The description must suffice to allow the client to properly consider the fees claimed. The Senior Costs Judge has summarised the law as follows:

> *"A bill must contain sufficient information to enable the client to obtain advice as to its detailed assessment".*[21]

3.52. Per Ward LJ in *Ralph Hume Garry (a firm) v Gwillim*[22] a bill will not be a statute bill if the client shows:

> *"i) that there is no sufficient narrative in the bill to identify what it is he is being charged for, and*
>
> *ii) that he does not have sufficient knowledge from other documents in his possession or from what he has been told reasonably to take advice whether or not to apply for that bill to be taxed."*

3.53. So, the sufficiency of the narrative is not the only question; the court must also look at whether the client's knowledge, whether gained from documents or advice given, is sufficient to allow him to take advice on whether to assess the bill (thus negating the need for a narrative).

3.54. In certain circumstances, a bill with a deficient narrative can still be a statute bill. In the *Garry* case the court did not interfere with the judge's decision below that *"Mr Ralph had shown a real prospect of establishing at the trial that Mr Gwillim knew all he needed to know about the work and the basis of charging reasonably to be able to exercise his right to seek taxation."*

3.55. In *Cook v Gillard*[23] Lord Campbell CJ put it thus:

---

21 Rahimian (1) Scandia Care Ltd (2) v Allan Janes LLP [2016] EWHC B18 (Costs) at [30]

22 [2002] EWCA Civ 1500 at [70]

23 (1852) 1 E&B 26. Cited with approval in *Garry* at [63]

"the defendant who undertakes to prove that the bill is not a bona fide compliance with the Act cannot found an objection upon want of information in the bill, if it appears that he is already in possession of that information ... a client has no ground of objection to a bill who is in possession of all the information that can be reasonably wanted for the consulting on taxation".

3.56. The preceding statements apply to contentious business. In the *Garry* case Ward LJ suggested that an alternative test (effectively excluding the question of the client's knowledge) which would apply to non-contentious business was an obiter comment and made without reference to the full authorities.[24] As a result, it is likely that the two-fold test applies to both contentious and non-contentious bills.

3.57. Of course, it would be a brave solicitor who sought to rely upon the client's knowledge to remedy an insufficient narrative. It is far better to ensure that the narrative is such that the client can properly ascertain what he is being charged for and make a decision as to whether to challenge the bill.

3.58. Whether a bill provides sufficient narrative for the client to ascertain what is being charged for and to enable him to seek advice should be obvious. As Erle J said in *Haigh v Ousey*[25]:

"Now I am sure no bill that contained charges for anything beyond mere steps in a cause ever did contain this full information. No person on earth by reading a bill of costs without further information can tell what is a fair charge for such an item as "advising you". It may have been a minute's work; it may have required a week's careful consideration. No man, unless there were interminable prolixity in the bill, could tell from the bill alone what is the fair charge for matters depending on the quantum meruit, that is, for almost everything except mere steps in a cause".

3.59. It would ordinarily be sufficient to ask oneself whether the information provided within the bill is such that, if the client passed it to

---

24 Denning LJ's comments in Re a Solicitor [1955] 2 QB 252.

25 (1857) 7 E&B 578

another solicitor or a costs lawyer, his new adviser could advise on whether the items are reasonable or whether they should be challenged.

3.60. Having recognised all of the above, it is open for a client to agree to forgo the narrative. In *Barclays PLC & Anor v Villers & Anor*[26] the court found that a lack of narrative did not render the statute bills mere request for payments on account since the lack of narrative was the result of a request from Barclays.

3.61. Langley J held that *"The common law 'rule' is for the benefit of the client and in my judgment the client can forego it if he so chooses"*.

3.62. One note of caution in respect of an agreement to forgo a narrative is that in the *Barclays* case the court found that the client was sophisticated and had all the information they needed through estimates provided. It is doubtful whether a court would so readily find that a client who is not sophisticated had agreed to forgo a narrative.

Complete

3.63. If a statute bill must enable the client to consider the fees (and allow them to consider whether to challenge them) then it follows that the bill must be reasonably complete. In addition, the court must be in a position to assess the bill. A partial bill would likely offend these principles.

3.64. As a rule of thumb, a final statute bill should be the complete bill of the charges levied under the retainer.

3.65. In *Cobbett v Wood*[27] the solicitors acted for the defendant's wife in divorce proceedings and recovered the costs of the petition. Those costs were assessed and paid. The solicitors then delivered a bill for the additional costs to their client headed "Costs as between solicitor and client, including costs not allowed as between party and party." This bill did not include any of the costs claimed or paid between the parties.

---

26 [2000] 1 All ER (Comm) 357 at pg 367

27 [1908] 2 KB 420

3.66. The solicitor began an action to recover the costs and the client argued that the bill was not a statute bill. The Court of Appeal agreed with the client. Per Farwell LJ:

> "I do not think that it is competent for a solicitor, where there has been a taxation of costs as between party and party, to deliver to the client a bill of the items not allowed on that taxation as a separate bill. The bill of fees, charges, and disbursements contemplated by s. 37 is, I think, a complete bill of the whole of the fees, charges, and disbursements in respect of the particular business done... Taxation as between solicitor and client necessitates the whole bill being before the Master, notwithstanding that it has already been taxed between party and party, and there is no reason why the fee should not be assessed on the whole bill thus submitted."

3.67. In this case the solicitor argued that, since the client had received the between the parties bill a year before, he could hunt down that bill and compare it to the new bill delivered. Farwell LJ did not accept this: "I agree with my brother Fletcher Moulton that probably he would not be able to do so, but in any case I do not think he is bound to do this in order to enable the solicitor to escape from his obligation to deliver a proper bill of costs".

3.68. In somewhat unusual circumstances Hobhouse LJ[28] has found that where a solicitor cannot include an item (and indeed it would be wrong to include it) in an initial bill then there is nothing objectionable about that first statute bill being assessed and then a second bill being delivered including that item, so long as the client is not being deceived when the first bill is raised.

3.69. In *Richard Slade & Co v Boodia*[29] the Court of Appeal held that a statute bill could comprise only profit costs or disbursements, so long as

---

28 Aaron v Okoye [1998] Costs LR 6- here the solicitor raised an initial bill but did not include counsel's fees as these were disputed and he was in discussion over their amount with counsel's clerk. Per para 2 of App 2 to Ord 62 those fees were not permitted to be allowed on assessment until they were agreed (and paid). The solicitor told the client (who was a member of the bar) that counsel's fee would not be included in the statute bill. It was assessed and then a further bill delivered. The client objected to the further bill on the basis that all costs should be included within the first bill.

the bill was complete and final in respect of the subject matter it covered.

3.70. The cases above do not negate the general principle that a statue bill should be reasonably complete and include all of the fees claimed under the retainer. They are best viewed as exceptions to the general rule.

Demand for Payment

3.71. A bill will not be a statute bill unless it is a demand for payment or a statement of what is due.

3.72. *Kingstons Solicitors v Reiss Solicitors*[30] concerned a firm of solicitors who had instructed solicitor agents to conduct work outside their expertise. A bill was sent attached to an email which read:

> *"I have attached a copy of the bill of costs. Just send it off as it is to the other side and let me know what they come back with. I have pitched it high deliberately so that it gives us some room to negotiate on the matter. In terms of how much for each person, we will sort that out at the end. Let us first see how much they are offering.".*

3.73. Tomlinson LJ held that the bill:

> *"...was not to be regarded by Reiss as the recipient as being a demand by Kingstons of Reiss for payment in the sum of £14,427.66. It represented no more than a document which had been produced with a view to assisting in the negotiations which Reiss were to have with the Treasury Solicitor regarding the recovery of costs as between party and party".* [32]

Errors and Omissions

3.74. Where a bill contains so many errors with the result that the assessing judge cannot properly assess the reasonableness of the charges it will need to be re-drafted properly and will lose its status as a statute bill.

---

30 [2014] EWCA Civ 172

3.75. In *Slingsby v Attorney-General* [31] the Master assessed a bill but the client appealed on the basis that the bill was so full of errors it should not have been assessed. The Court of Appeal agreed. Per Swinfen-Eady J:

> *"In the present case the bill of costs has been improperly made out, and the taxing officer has not had before him the proper material upon which he could reasonably exercise his discretion. It is made out by including in general terms, and sometimes specifically, a large number of details which are obviously wrong. It is only one lump sum charged, but a large number of details are obviously erroneous, which ought not to be included in the costs... There will have to be another taxation now upon a new bill of costs. The bill will have to be remodelled and carried in in the right form. There will be a wholly new taxation".*

3.76. However, simply because a bill contains items in error (or items which could not be recovered) does not mean the bill cannot be assessed. The solicitor can seek the residue of the costs[32].

3.77. These two statements may appear to conflict at first glance; they do not. In the first instance the court was unable to properly assess the bill by virtue of the errors. In the second, the court could remove the items that were not capable of justification and assess the residue. The question is whether the errors and format of the bill allow the costs judge to assess the items claimed; if so the errors may sound in costs but will not mean the bill is rejected; if not a new bill will need to be prepared.[33]

Finality of Statute Bills

3.78. In a between the parties assessment the receiving party can serve a bill and then amend it without requiring permission. This is not the case in solicitor and client assessments under the Act.

---

31 [1918-19] All ER Rep 239

32 Pilgrim v Hirschfeld (1863) 3 New Rep 36

33 And in those circumstances, the timescales under the Act would run from delivery of the new bill.

3.79. Save in two circumstances, and subject to the exception of gross sum bills set out below, once a solicitor delivers his statute bill he cannot subsequently amend or substitute it for a new bill.

3.80. Amendment or substitution is only possible where either (a) the client consents or (b) the court so orders. This has been long established. In *Saad v Griffin*[34] Farwell LJ stated:

> "... it is settled beyond controversy that the solicitor is, for the purposes of taxation, bound by the bill that he has delivered and cannot alter it without the leave of the Court or the consent of the party."

(a) The Consent of the Client

3.81. It had been argued that only the court could provide for the substitution or amendment a statute bill. In *Rezvi v Brown Cooper (a firm)*[35] Newman J rejected this proposition and found that a client can consent to the withdrawal of a bill.

3.82. The client can consent explicitly, but the court may also find that the client's consent can be implied. For example, in *Rezvi* the court held that when the client sought assessment of the second substituted bill, he consented to the substitution of that bill for the first.

3.83. Even where the client consents to a fresh bill this does not mean that the original is disregarded. The court may have regard to the original when assessing the costs.

(b) If the Court Orders

3.84. In *Polak v Marchioness of Winchester*[36] when the solicitor's bill came before the judge on assessment they noticed that counsel's fees had not been paid (and were not therefore allowable). They sought an adjournment so that they could pay counsel and then submit a fresh bill for assessment.

---

34 [1928] 2 KB 510

35 [1997] Costs LR 109

36 [1956] 2 All ER 660

3.85. The omission had been a mistake and *'an unfortunate oversight'* (the court commented that it did not reflect well on the firm's office administration). At first instance the judge allowed the amendment finding that *"the omission to pay these fees was due to bona fide mistake and inadvertence, and that there was no intention whatever on the part of the solicitors to do anything dishonest in the matter, or to overreach the client in any way"*. The client appealed arguing, inter-alia, that the court had no jurisdiction to make the order.

3.86. The Court of Appeal upheld the decision and dismissed the appeal. Per Jenkins LJ:

(i) *"the learned judge in the court below had jurisdiction to make the order sought"*. (667)

(ii) *"It is only in exceptional cases, cases of special circumstances, of genuine mistake or inadvertence, that assistance ought to be given"*. (668)

(iii) But he cautioned: *"one has to take a strict view to maintain the necessary safeguards, and nothing that I say is to be regarded as suggesting to solicitors that they can be careless or un-business like in a matter such as this, and then, as of course, apply for and receive the assistance of the court"*. (667)

3.87. As can be seen, the circumstances where the court will allow the amendment or substitution of a statute bill are likely to be few.

Gross Sum Bills

3.88. An exception to the finality of a bill is the situation where a gross sum bill is delivered to a client and the client, under the Act, seeks a detailed bill.

3.89. The Act sets out the provisions in s.64:

"(1) Where the remuneration of a solicitor in respect of contentious business done by him is not the subject of a contentious business agreement, then, subject to subsections (2) to (4), the solicitor's bill of costs may at the option of the solicitor be either a bill containing detailed items or a gross sum bill.

(2) The party chargeable with a gross sum bill may at any time—

(a) before he is served with a writ or other originating process for the recovery of costs included in the bill, and

(b) before the expiration of three months from the date on which the bill was delivered to him, require the solicitor to deliver, in lieu of that bill, a bill containing detailed items; and on such a requirement being made the gross sum bill shall be of no effect.

(3) Where an action is commenced on a gross sum bill, the court shall, if so requested by the party chargeable with the bill before the expiration of one month from the service on that party of the writ or other originating process, order that the bill be assessed.

(4) If a gross sum bill is assessed whether under this section or otherwise, nothing in this section shall prejudice any rules of court with respect to assessment, and the solicitor shall furnish the costs officer with such details of any of the costs covered by the bill as the costs officer may require."

3.90. The effect of a request by the client within the specified time period is that the detailed bill replaces the gross sum bill and the solicitor is perfectly within his rights to deliver a detailed bill which is for a higher sum.

3.91. If the client wishes to have a gross sum bill assessed but does not want to risk a higher replacement bill he can seek the assessment and the court will ordinarily give directions which require a breakdown of the costs (setting out the items in a format which mean the costs judge may assess them).

3.92. The standard directions at r.46.10 (2) specifies that a court will order that:

"The solicitor must serve a breakdown of costs within 28 days of the order for costs to be assessed."

3.93. Thus, a client in receipt of a gross sum bill who wishes to have a detailed breakdown could simply seek an assessment and ask the court to order the solicitor to prepare one. The advantage of that, as opposed to a request under s.64 of the Act, is that the bill amount stays the same (whatever the breakdown adds up to).

3.94. It is important that a client who seeks clarification as to a gross sum bill does not inadvertently invoke s.64. In *Carlton v Theodore Goddard & Co*[37] a gross sum bill was delivered and the client sought its assessment writing *"Accordingly, it would seem that there is no alternative but for your bill to be prepared and lodged for taxation."*

3.95. The solicitors argued that this was a request under s.64[38] and enabled them to replace the gross sum bill with a higher detailed bill. The court disagreed with Megarry J stating:

> *"First, then, there is the question whether the plaintiff ever required the defendants to deliver to him in lieu of the gross sum bill "a bill containing detailed items." I cannot see that he has…It seems to me that before proviso (a) of section 64 is brought into play there must be something which can fairly be described as a request or requirement that the solicitors should deliver to the client a detailed bill to replace the gross sum bill already delivered; and although I do not think that any particular form of words need be employed, the substance of what is relied upon must amount to a request or requirement of this kind. If in doubt, of course, the solicitors, before embarking on the work, can always inquire whether some equivocal communication that they have received is or is not intended to be a requirement under the proviso. On this ground alone the defendants' contentions must fail."*

3.96. To avoid disputes, solicitors would be advised to ensure that before a gross sum bill is replaced (a) the client has explicitly asked for a detailed breakdown per s.64 and (b) if there is any ambiguity in the request the client is asked to clarify what it is they seek.

3.97. For clients, it would ordinarily be unwise to risk seeking a replacement bill under the Act. The only advantage in not waiting for the court to order a breakdown would be where the client wishes to avoid litigation and deal with the matter without proceedings.

---

37 [1973] 1 WLR 623

38 This was s.64 of the Solicitors Act 1957 but it is in identical terms to the current s.64.

Conditional Bills

3.98. A solicitor may in certain limited circumstances deliver a statute bill on the condition that it may be amended.

3.99. In *Re: Thompson*[39] Cotton LJ summarised the position of the solicitors in that case thus: *"We sent our bill in under a condition that if it was not paid within eight days we should be at liberty to withdraw it; it was not paid and we withdrew it, and sent in this new bill."*

3.100. Lindley LJ made it clear that it a solicitor could deliver a bill with conditions (453) but only if the client was treated fairly. The judge found in that case:

> *"Messrs. Thompson knew, so far as I can see from the evidence, that that bill was not an honest bill - not a bill by which they were prepared to stand at all. It was not a bill as to which they could safely or fairly say to their client, "This is our bill made up to the best of our ability; it contains charges which you may pay if you are disposed, but which we tell you frankly we are not prepared to maintain." Any honest disclosure of that sort would have made all the difference in the world; but when we find that the contrary was the fact, and that the bill was one which they must have thought or hoped would be treated by the client as fairly made out - when it was not - it appears to me that they have not fulfilled their obligation as solicitors to their client, in expressing the condition in the language which they did".*

3.101. The solicitor in that case was delivering a bill on conditions which amounted to them reserving the right to put in a different bill if it was not paid. Further, the bill itself was not capable of justification at assessment.

3.102. In those circumstances the court will not allow the condition to permit the solicitor to withdraw the bill. The assessment must be on the basis of the statute bill delivered.

3.103. If the solicitor treats the client fairly and properly and clearly explains the condition (and why it is required) then the court may permit conditional delivery. As *Re: Thompson* shows, the court is most unlikely

---

39 (1885) 30 ChD 441

to do so where the condition benefits the solicitor to the determent of the client.

CHAPTER FOUR
INTERIM STATUE BILLS

Introduction

4.1. A solicitor will usually deliver a statute bill at the end of the retainer. This is a final statute bill. However, it is possible to deliver interim statute bills throughout the currency of the retainer. These are statute bills that must comply with all of the requirements set out in Chapter Three and are identical to final statute bills save that they cover a specified period of time.

4.2. Spencer J in *Bari v Rosen (t/a Rosen Solicitors)1* explained the concept as follows:

> "...*a solicitor may contract with his client for the right to issue statute bills from time to time during the currency of the retainer. Such bills are known as "interim statute bills". They are nevertheless final bills in respect of the work they cover, in that there can be no subsequent adjustment in the light of the outcome of the business. They are complete self-contained bills of costs to date*". [15]

4.3. Why would a solicitor want to deliver interim statute bills? At first glance, there are a number of downsides. They are final bills for the period covered and cannot ordinarily be substituted or amended so the solicitor must ensure that the sums billed during the work are correct. If the solicitor simply wishes to be put in funds then he can deliver bills on account (seeking payments on account) and does not need to deliver interim statute bills at all.

4.4. For the client there are also disadvantages; the timescales under the Act run from the delivery of each interim statute bill and so the client may need to consider whether to challenge the costs while their solicitor is continuing to act for them. Understandably, the client's focus is likely to be on the action itself and they may not wish to upset the relationship with their solicitor. Master Leonard has put it thus:

---

1 [2012] 5 Costs LR 851

"The potential difficulties and expense faced by a client who can only challenge regular bills by instituting multiple assessment proceedings - against the same solicitor who is actively handling a number of current matter for him - are obvious. Further, the choice is between a right which begins to diminish after one month from the first regular bill and a right which does not begin to diminish until a later and, for the client, obviously more practicable time."[2]

4.5. The main advantage of interim statute bills is certainty. The solicitor and the client will reach the end of the retainer knowing that the fees have been paid.

4.6. When the issue of interim statute bills arises within solicitor and client disputes it is usually within the context of a client wishing to challenge the fees. If the solicitor asserts that interim statute bills have been delivered (rather than bills on account) the client is likely to be out of time to challenge many of the bills[3].

4.7. The court must ask two questions:

(i) Is the solicitor entitled to deliver interim statute bills?

(ii) If so, can the bills themselves be classified as statute bills?

4.8. As Spencer J said in *Bari*:

"Even if there was a contractual right to issue interim statute bills, it would be a question of fact whether any individual bill issued to the client was a statute bill. If there was no contractual entitlement to issue an interim statute bill, any interim bill issued could be no more than a request for payment on account". [17]

4.9. As can be seen, the right to render interim statute bills does not mean that any bills delivered have that status. Both criteria must be satisfied.

---

2 Cited in *Bari v Rosen* (an appeal from Master Leonard) at [29]

3 See Chapter Five

An Entire Contract

4.10. As explained in Chapter One, save in the circumstances set out below, a solicitor's retainer is an entire contract and the fees for the work undertaken cannot be sought until the end of the work or where the retainer has been lawfully terminated[4].

4.11. Thus, in the ordinary course of events and absent the circumstances discussed below, there is no right to bill a client during the currency of a retainer.

When Can a Solicitor Deliver an Interim Statute Bills?

4.12. A solicitor may deliver an interim statute bill where there is an agreement (whether express or implied) to do so or where there is a natural break in the litigation.

(i) Express Agreement

4.13. Arguments about express agreements almost always involve the court analysing the retainer document and considering whether it provides for the delivery of interim statute bills.

4.14. This is because, as has been seen, where there is a dispute over retainer which has not been put in writing then, all things being equal, the client's word is to be preferred over the solicitor.[5]

4.15. Therefore, as a general rule, if a solicitor seeks to argue that there is an agreement to deliver interim statute bills and the client disagrees, where the agreement has not been put in writing the client's view will triumph. The lesson here is simple; if interim statute bills are required then the solicitor should ensure the retainer sets this out clearly.

4.16. The senior courts have repeatedly made clear that if a solicitor does wish to render interim statute bills he must make it plain that the

---

4 See *Bari v Rosen* at [15]

5 See 1.5 above

bills sent have this status. Roskill LJ commented in *Davidsons v Jones-Fenleigh*[6]:

> "...*a solicitor is entitled to select a point of time which he regards an appropriate point of time at which to send in a bill. But before he is entitled to require that bill to be treated as a complete self-contained bill of costs to date, he must make it plain to the client either expressly or by necessary implication that that is his purpose of sending in that bill for that amount at that time*".

4.17. Fulford J put it thus in *Adams v Al- Malik*[7]:

> "*In particular the party must know what rights are being negotiated and dispensed with in the sense that the solicitor must make it plain to the client that the purpose of sending the bill at that time is that it is to be treated as a complete self-contained bill of costs to date*". [48]

4.18. Many disputes arising from potential interim statute bills centre on the wording within the retainer. If the court finds that there are ambiguities or that the retainer, properly read as a whole, does not support the view that the solicitor 'made it plain' to the client that interim statute bills were being delivered then the bills will be found to be no more than requests for payments on account.

4.19. As with all contracts, the court will interpret the terms of the contractual retainer by reference to the agreement as a whole and give effect to the presumed intention of the agreement, construed objectively by reference to the factual matrix at the time of the agreement. The parties' subjective intentions are not relevant.[8]

4.20. In *Bari v Rosen* the retainer letter provided that:

> "*I shall send you a regular statutory final bill, which will not be altered subsequently... I require payment of the bill by return and will argue about any aspect of the charges subsequently. You have a right to have an assessment of my bills at any time in the High Court.*

---

6   (1980) Costs LR 70

7   [2014] 6 Costs LR 985

8   See *Bari v Rosen* at [21]

Ask for details from me at any time.…Apart from that, all bills are self-contained. You and I will agree that each such subsequent bill is fair and reasonable when billed. The bills are for acceptance; but I do reserve my rights to charge as and when appropriate. You must pay any disbursements of any kind. I am not prepared to disburse out. All disbursements will be supported by a bill or record of indebtedness" [18]

4.21. The High Court upheld the costs judge's finding that this retainer did not provide for interim statute bills to be delivered. This was because the wording of the retainer was ambiguous in that it seemingly provided for interim statute bills to be delivered but then told the client that he had a right to have them assessed 'at any time.' Clearly, under the Act the timescales for assessment flow from the date of delivery and so, if these were statute bills, the client could not assess them at any time; quite the contrary.

4.22. In *Vlamaki v Sookias & Sookias*[9] the High Court again upheld a costs judge's decision that a series of bills were not interim statute bills because of the wording of the retainer. Walker J accepted a concession properly made by the solicitor's counsel that:

"if there were an ambiguity on a fundamental aspect of the terms and conditions that cannot otherwise be resolved then the ambiguity is to be determined against the solicitors." [15]

4.23. In this case the retainer provided that:

"6.1 To help you budget, we will send you a bill for our charges and expenses at the end of each month while the work is in progress. We will send you a final bill after completion of the work.

6.2. If not paid from monies on account, payment is due to us on delivery of a bill. We reserve the right to charge you interest on the bill at 4% over the base rate prevailing from time to time from the date of the bill if you do not pay our bill within this time …" [14]

---

9 [2015] EWHC 3334 (QB)

4.24. The judge upheld the decision below that the reference to sending the client a final bill was ambiguous because, as the judge below had said:

> *"It can be asked rhetorically, why, if all bills were statute bills, is it necessary to say that a final bill will be sent unless all the previous bills were not final but something else, namely interim on account of a final bill?"* [18]

4.25. The fact that interest was to be levied on the bills was not found to be determinative with Walker J finding:

> *"I do not underestimate the force of the argument that they must be statute bills because of what is said in the retainer as to payment being due and as to interest. That argument, however, assumes knowledge of the 1974 Act and procedures under it: but this does not sit happily with (the) concession... In the ordinary course a lay client cannot be assumed to have such knowledge".* [23]

4.26. As to the terms of the retainer, the judge noted:

> *"Absent from those clauses in particular and the retainer in general is any express statement that each interim bill would be a final bill for the period that it covered".* [23]

4.27. How should the retainer express an agreement to deliver interim statute bills? Put simply, the wording should be clear, unambiguous and explain plainly what the effect of sending those bills is.

4.28. If a solicitor wishes to deliver such bills the following wording is suggested:

(i) Billing and Payment

1. We will send you bills of costs every month during the retainer. These will be final statute bills for the period they cover and must be paid within 7 days of receipt. We will charge interest at the rate of 4% above the prevailing Bank of England base rate in respect of bills which are not paid within 7 days of receipt.

2. Please note that the bills we send you will not simply be requests for payments on account. They are the final charges for the

period they cover and will stand as our fees. They will not be amended or substituted.

3. If you wish to challenge the amount of the bills you should note the timescales set out within the Solicitors Act 1974 at s.70. This provides that you have an absolute right to seek an assessment of our costs by the court within one month of delivery of the bill. Thereafter, you may seek an assessment within 12 months but if you have paid the bill you will be required to show special circumstances. If you wait for more than 12 months after paying the bill you will lose the right to have our fees assessed.

4. You should not wait until the end of the matter before challenging our fees. You should consider each bill when it is sent and if you wish to challenge the fees or have the court assess them this must be done at the point at which you receive each bill.

5. We hope that this is clear but if you have any questions about billing arrangements or the effect of us delivering statute bills please speak to Mr/Ms/Mrs XXXX who will be happy to explain matter further".

(ii) Implied Agreement

4.29. The court may also consider the conduct of the client when the bills are received and can infer that there is an agreement that the bills are to be treated as interim statute bills. Bowen LJ explained that even if the solicitor had no right to deliver interim statute bills:

"... we must ask ourselves the further question of fact whether both parties agreed to treat the documents as bills delivered under the Act."[10]

4.30. In *Davidsons v Jones-Fenleigh* Roskill LJ commented that, once a solicitor had sent what purports to be an interim statute bill one should consider the actions of the client:

---

10 In re Romer & Haslam (1893) 2 QB 286

"If the client's reaction is to pay the bill in its entirety without demur it is not difficult to infer an agreement that that bill is to be treated as a complete self contained bill of costs to date..."

4.31. In that case the judge concluded that:

"...there was a clear intention on the part of the appellants, and indeed a plain agreement to be inferred from the conduct of the parties that those bills should be treated as completely self-contained bills covering the period down to the relevant date given".

4.32. That said, the mere fact that bills have been paid does not, in and of itself, automatically mean that the court will infer an agreement that they be treated as interim statute bills[11]. Bills paid under protest (or with the client making it clear that they will have them assessed at the end of the retainer) will weigh against a finding that the bills are statute bills. All the circumstances of the delivery and payment will be considered when the court weighs up whether there was an implied agreement.

4.33. It is an obvious point that it is preferable for the retainer to set out clearly that interim statute bills will be delivered. As noted, when the court is considering differing interpretations of agreements not reduced to writing the client's view is likely to be preferred.

(iii) Natural Break

4.34. As Simon Brown LJ has noted[12]:

"There is authority for the rendering of an interim bill at a natural break in protracted litigation. There is, however, little authority in identifying what is a natural break".

4.35. Denning LJ in *Chamberlain v Boodle and King (a firm)*[13] commented:

"...it is a question of fact whether there are natural breaks in the work done by a solicitor so that each portion of it can and should be

---

11 See Abedi v Penningtons (a firm) [2000] All ER (D) 383

12 Abedi v Penningtons (a firm) [2000] All ER (D) 383

13 [1982] 3 All ER 188

treated as a separate and distinct part in itself, capable of and rightly being charged separately and taxed separately."

4.36. It is rare for a retainer to specify a natural break in the proceedings when a statute bill could be delivered and as a result the issue most frequently arises as an argument to support an implied agreement for the rendering of an interim statute bill.

4.37. Lord Esher[14] has defined a natural break as the *"conclusion of a definite and distinct part of the legal transaction as would entitle the solicitors to send in a final bill of costs."*

4.38. Whether there is a natural break in the proceedings will be fact specific. Denning LJ found held in *Chamberlain* that there was no natural break commenting:

> *"...it seems to me that over this short time, the end of November 1978 to the beginning of May 1979, this was one continuous dealing and work done by a solicitor, not dividing itself naturally or otherwise into any breaks at all".*

4.39. As with an implied agreement, if a solicitor wishes to render an interim statute bill at certain points in the proceedings it is preferable for this to be clearly stated and explained within the retainer. This will avoid arguments about whether, in the specific circumstances, a natural break arose which allowed a statute bill to be delivered.

Chamberlain Bills

4.40. If the solicitor has delivered a series of bills during a retainer, and those bills have been found to be mere requests for payments on account rather than interim statute bills, there is a potential disadvantage for the client. Before considering whether to challenge the fees they will have to await a final statute bill (which could be higher than the total of those previously sent). Moreover, the client may wish to assess the costs straight away but cannot do so until the final statute bill is delivered.

4.41. One solution is for a judge to find that the bills delivered throughout the retainer are a series of bills culminating with a final bill. This is a 'Chamberlain' bill – so called because the concept was first es-

---

14 In re Romer & Haslam (1893) 2 QB 286

poused by Denning LJ in *Chamberlain v Boodle and King (a firm)*. In that case the court was concerned with 4 bills and found that there was no natural break to allow interim statute bills to be delivered. Denning LJ found:

> *"When the bills were delivered, they were delivered each time as part of the running account - 'account rendered' being carried on in each to the next. I agree with the judge ... that this should be regarded as one bill in respect of one complete piece of work, although divided into parts. As this is one bill, and the client demanded taxation within the month, he is entitled to have the whole of it taxed."*

4.42. A Chamberlain bill has significant advantages for the client. As it is one statute bill (comprised of the original bills) the amounts cannot ordinarily be amended or substituted for greater sums. Equally as important, the date of delivery of the bill for the purposes of the timescales under the Act runs from the date of delivery of the final in the series, not the date when each individual bill was delivered. The effect of this is that the client will not be out of time for challenging the earlier bills. The entire set of bills will be assessed.

4.43. This type of bill will never be intentional. As Spencer J said in *Bari v Rosen "Whilst no solicitor would set out to create such a series of bills, it does happen."*

4.44. Where such a bill is found to have been created the original bills do not become statute bills. Indeed, a Chamberlain bill would not be required if the original bills had that status. Master Leonard explained the point this way:

> *"The second primary submission is that my conclusion that all the bills rendered to the claimant can be treated as a series concluding with the final bill of January 2010, is inconsistent with my finding that the pre-22 January 2010 bills are not statute bills. That seems to me to overlook the distinction between individual bills and a series of bills. An individually incomplete bill may form part of a complete series. A series of non-statute bills may be treated a series culminating in one final statute bill"*[15]

---

15 Cited with approval in *Bari v Rosen* at [55]

4.45. Where a client argues that bills delivered are not interim statute bills they should ordinarily seek to argue that the bills should be considered a Chamberlain bill; that would usually be preferable to an order for delivery up of a final statute bill.

Are the Bills Statute Bills?

4.46. As stated above, once the court finds that the solicitor had a right to deliver interim statute bills the question is whether the actual bills delivered have that status.

4.47. Readers should refer to Chapter Three for the requirements of a statute bill. All of those requirements apply as much to interim statute bills as they do to final statute bills.

CHAPTER FIVE
APPLYING FOR AN
ASSESSMENT

Introduction

5.1 This chapter will consider the timescales under the Act and who may seek an assessment of costs.

Timescales

5.2. The right of the party chargeable to have a bill assessed diminishes with time. In certain circumstances the right to have an assessment under the Act ceases altogether.

5.3. This explains why the issues of whether a bill is a statute bill and when it has been delivered is so important. The delivery of a statue bill or an interim statute bill starts the timescales under the Act.

5.4. The paragraphs below assume that a bone fide statute bill has been delivered in accordance with the Act.

Definitions of One Month and Twelve Months

5.5. It will often be crucial to establish whether there have been proceedings issued for assessment of or for recovery of fees within the timescales allowed by the Act.

5.6. The Act speaks of 'one month' and 'twelve months'. The Interpretation Act 1978 at Schedule One[1] states: "Month" means calendar month.

5.7. *Blunt v Heslop*[2] is a case from 1838 but still appears to be good law. This establishes that when calculating the timescales one excludes the date of delivery and the day when the action is commenced.

---

1 https://www.legislation.gov.uk/ukpga/1978/30/schedule/1

2 (1838) 4 A & E 577

Prior to One Month

(i) The Solicitor

5.8. Ordinarily a solicitor must wait for one month from delivery of their bill before they bring an action for the recovery of their fees. The Act at s.69 provides two circumstances when a solicitor may commence proceedings before the expiration of a month. It provides:

> *"Subject to the provisions of this Act, no action shall be brought to recover any costs due to a solicitor before the expiration of one month from the date on which a bill of those costs is delivered in accordance with the requirements mentioned in subsection (2); but if there is probable cause for believing that the party chargeable with the costs —*

> *(a) is about to quit England and Wales, to become bankrupt or to compound with his creditors, or*

> *(b) is about to do any other act which would tend to prevent or delay the solicitor obtaining payment"*

5.9. This allows the solicitor to commence an action for the recovery of fees almost immediately where they are at risk of the client being unable to meet any judgment obtained.

5.10. If the party chargeable seeks an assessment of the fees within one month of the delivery of the bill then the court will order that no action will be commenced by the solicitor in respect of recovery of the fees until the assessment is completed. S.70 (1) of the Act provides:

> *"Where before the expiration of one month from the delivery of a solicitor's bill an application is made by the party chargeable with the bill, the High Court shall, without requiring any sum to be paid into court, order that the bill be assessed and that no action be commenced on the bill until the assessment is completed".*

(ii) The Client

5.11. As can be seen, s.70(1) provides a complete and unfettered right of the party chargeable with the bill to have an assessment of the costs. No conditions may be attached to the order for assessment.

After One Month but Before Twelve Months

5.12. The Act at s.70(2)(a) and (b) provides:

> *"Where no such application is made before the expiration of the period mentioned in subsection (1), then, on an application being made by the solicitor or, subject to subsections (3) and (4), by the party chargeable with the bill, the court may on such terms, if any, as it thinks fit (not being terms as to the costs of the assessment), order—*
>
> *(a) that the bill be assessed; and*
>
> *(b) that no action be commenced on the bill, and that any action already commenced be stayed, until the assessment is completed".*

5.13. The solicitor or the party chargeable may seek an assessment after one month has expired. If the application is issued prior to twelve months after the bill is delivered the court will have a complete discretion to allow the assessment but may do so on conditions.

5.14. In practice, the court will order an assessment where the application is made within this timescale however, it is not unusual for the solicitor to seek a payment on account of costs at the same time.

5.15. Additionally, the court will order that any existing action for the recovery of fees be stayed if already commended or will order that no action be begun by the solicitor to recover the fees. If assessment proceedings are commenced after the solicitor has sued for his fees is it imperative that the client seeks such an order at the outset.

After Twelve Months Where the Bill has not been Paid

5.16. The Act at s.70(3)(a) and (b) covers the situation where the party chargeable seeks assessment of the bill after twelve months has elapsed from delivery.

5.17. The statute provides:

> "*Where an application under subsection (2) is made by the party chargeable with the bill—*
>
> *(a) after the expiration of 12 months from the delivery of the bill, or*
>
> *(b) after a judgment has been obtained for the recovery of the costs covered by the bill,*
>
> *...no order shall be made except in special circumstances and, if an order is made, it may contain such terms as regards the costs of the assessment as the court may think fit".*

5.18. Thus, if the party chargeable seeks an assessment after twelve months or after a judgment has been obtained (in an action to recover the fees brought by the solicitor) then the court may only order that there be an assessment if the party chargeable can show special circumstances. Such an order can be made on conditions (again, the most usual one being that the client makes a payment on account of the fees).

After the Bill has been paid but before Twelve Months
from the payment

5.19. Per s.70(3)(c) the party chargeable will need to show special circumstances where an application is made to assess a bill that has been paid (but where the application is made before the expiry of twelve months from the payment).

After Twelve Months from the date of payment

5.20. There is an absolute cut off point within the Act. Once the party chargeable has paid the bill if no application for assessment is made within twelve months of that payment the court cannot order an assessment under any circumstances.[3]

5.21. This is set out in s.70(4):

> *"The power to order assessment conferred by subsection (2) shall not be exercisable on an application made by the party chargeable with the bill after the expiration of 12 months from the payment of the bill".*

Table of Timescales

5.22. the table below sets out the relevant timescales in summary:

One month after delivery of the Bill **Absolute Right to Assessment**	The party chargeable may make an application for assessment of the bill and the court **will** order that the bill be assessed (without conditions). No action may be taken for recovery of the costs until the assessment is completed
After one month after delivery but before twelve months **Discretionary Right to Assessment**	The court **may** make an order for assessment (and in practice will do so)but with conditions and may order that no action be commenced to recover the fees (and any action begun be held in abeyance) until the assessment is completed.

---

3 However, while the right to an assessment under the Act is irrevocably lost, the client may still be entitled to a non-statutory assessment – see Chaopter Seven.

• After twelve months from the delivery of the Bill • After judgment has been obtained for the recovery of costs covered by the Bill • After the Bill has been paid but before the expiration of twelve months from the payment of the Bill **Special Circumstances Required**	No order shall be made expect in special circumstances
More than twelve months after the Bill is paid **No Right of Assessment**	The court **cannot** make an order for assessment

<u>Date of Delivery</u>

5.23. Delivery is dealt with in Chapter Three. For the purposes of this chapter it is worth re-iterating that:

(i) If interim statute bills are delivered the timescales run from the date of delivery of each bill.

(ii) If the court finds that a Chamberlain bill exists, the date of delivery will be the date of the final bill in the series.

Payment

5.24. Whether a bill has been paid is of huge importance when considering the timescales under the Act. It is worth noting that the court's ability to order an assessment is only completely curtailed where there has been payment of a bill.

Part Payment

5.25. Where a bill is paid in part, that will not be taken as payment for the purposes of the Act.[4]

Deduction

5.26. There will be circumstances where payment is taken by the solicitor from funds he holds. The key question for the purposes of the Act is whether the client is aware of or has knowledge of the payment.

5.27. Considering deductions and whether these amounted to payments under the Act, in *Re Jackson*[5] Rowlatt J said:

> *"Payment is an operation in which two parties take part. If a man collects a debt due to his debtor and purports to pay his own debt in that way, it is not really a payment unless the other party knows what is being done and agrees that the sum received in that way by his creditor shall be used in the payment of his debt".*

5.28. The consequence of this is that where a deduction is made with the client's full knowledge this can result in payment under the Act[6].

5.29. In *Rippon Patel and French LLP v Mowlam*[7] the client sought an assessment more than twelve months after the bill had been delivered. The solicitor argued that no assessment could take place because the bill had been paid more than twelve months before the application. The client argued that the bill had only been paid in part.

5.30. Here, the solicitor had delivered a bill for the sum of £65,000 plus VAT and the matter had settled at mediation for a costs inclusive sum. During the mediation, the solicitors had said that they would settle the costs for £65,000 (and did not mention VAT). The firm had taken the £65,000 from the settlement sum and kept £13,000 in the

---

4 Re: Woodard (1869) 18 WR 37

5 [1915] 1 KB 371 at 383

6 See Forsinard Estates v Dykes [1971] 1 WLR 237 per Stamp J

7 [2020] EWHC 1079 (QB)

client account (relating to VAT).

5.31. At first instance the costs judge found that there had not been 'payment' of the bill under the Act, as the client had not agreed to or paid the VAT element. This decision was upheld by Eady J.

5.32. The *Rippon* case highlights how important it is for solcitors to be very clear as to what element of a global sum relates to costs. Further, it re-iterates the point that where a bill is said to be paid via a deduction of funds held, the client must be fully aware of the situation.

Payment made long before a bill is delivered

5.33. The courts have found that where payment has been taken and a bill delivered afterwards then so long as the payments are referable to the bill in question it can be said that payment has been made. Per Charles J:

> "…where a bill of costs is delivered after payment, if the payment can be referred to the bill of costs, an order for taxation will not be made. Here the payment can clearly be referred to the subsequently delivered bill of costs".[8]

5.34. Of course, the key point in the above instance is that a statute bill had subsequently been delivered. If there is no statute bill at all then there can be no payment. Lord Romilly made this clear in *In Re Street*[9]:

> "I have held over and over again that there can be no payment, within the meaning of the 41st section of the Act, before the bill has been delivered, and before the client has had the opportunity of seeing the items. If a solicitor sells an estate, receives the purchase-money, deducts the amount of his costs, and pays the balance to the client, that is not payment within the 41st section, if he has not delivered his bill of costs".

---

8   In Re R.G. Thompson ex parte Baylis [1894] 1 Q.B. 462 at pg 465

9   (1870) L. R. 10 Eq. 165

Special Circumstances

5.35. In *Falmouth House Freehold Co Ltd v Morgan Walker LLP*[10] Lewison J said this:

> *"Whether special circumstances exist is essentially a value judgment. It depends on comparing the particular case with the run of the mill case, in order to decide whether a detailed assessment in the particular case is justified despite the restrictions contained in s 70(3)"* [13]

5.36. Due to the nature of the value judgment, appellant courts will be slow to interfere with a decision of a costs judge at first instance. In *Re: Hirst & Capes*[11] Vaughan Williams LJ commented:

> *"No one now says that "special circumstances" must necessarily be circumstances of fraud, dishonest practice, or extortion, or anything of that kind. ...inasmuch as the Legislature has not in the Solicitors Act, 1843, given any definition of "special circumstances," they must refuse to formulate any such definition; but it is also plain that, although the question whether there are special circumstances is one for the exercise of the judge's discretion in each particular case, the discretion which he has so to exercise is a judicial discretion; and, if a Court of Appeal think that in what he has decided he has clearly not exercised a Judicial discretion, they may overrule his decision, but otherwise they will not interfere with it".*

5.37. Thus, it is not possible to set out a definitive list of special circumstances; each case will turn on its own fact and the decision of the judge will be based upon considering all the circumstances. The examples below are not an exhaustive list.

5.38. In terms of the definition of 'special circumstances' the words in the Act mean what they say; there is no requirement to show 'exceptional circumstances.'[12]

---

10 [2010] EWHC 3092 (Ch)

11 [1908] 1 K.B. 982 pg 990

12 Wilsons Solicitors v Bentine [2015] EWCA Civ 1168 per Sales LJ at [69]

5.39. Although the court will deal with submissions as to special circumstances individually, if there is more than one then the court should also have regard to their combined or cumulative effect.[13] As Michael Briggs QC (sitting as a Deputy high Court Judge) put it:

> "the question whether special circumstances are or not shown in any particular case requires an assessment of the aggregate of the relevant circumstances rather than an item by item assessment of each one"[14]

5.40. When considering whether special circumstances has been shown the court can take into account the fact that the paying party is a sophisticated client. In *Ingrams & Anor v Sykes*,[15] when rejecting a submission that special circumstances should be found, Donaldson MR took into account the fact that the party chargeable were:

> "experienced litigators…advised by experienced solicitors."

Examples

Unreasonably Large Bill, Excessive Costs or Gross Errors

5.41. Where the costs claimed within the bill are wholly excessive or include items which could not be justified special circumstances may be made out. In *In Re G.B.B Norman*[16] Lord Esher found that *"the amount of the charges is very large, almost frightful"*. The client rather than the solicitor had paid money to the witnesses and the solicitor had claimed for an in-house shorthand writer as though he were a professional. The judge concluded:

> "To sum up the material facts, there were very large bills of costs, a gross blunder, and a very extraordinary charge: these circumstances do amount to "special circumstances" within the meaning of the statute, and I think that the bills of costs ought to be taxed".

---

13 See Kris Motor Spares v Fox Williams LLP [2009] 6 Costs LR 931 at [103]

14 Arrowfield Services Limited v B P Collins (a firm) [2003] EWHC 830 (Ch) at [9]

15 137 NLJ 1135

16 (1886) 16 Q.B.D. 673

5.42. In *Re Robinson*[17] the court found that *"an unusual charge of a large amount requiring explanation to justify it"* amounted to special circumstances.

5.43. However, if the bill appears at first glance excessive but the solicitor is able to justify the fees then this will not amount to special circumstances. In *Winchester Commodities Group Ltd v RD Black & Co*[18] John Martin QC (sitting as a Deputy High Court Judge) rejected an argument that the bills were so excessive as to require an explanation. Having found that *"on the face of it the fees do seems extremely high"* the judge listed seven explanations provided by the solicitor and held:

> *"Viewed in the light of those seven factors, it seems to me that what at first sight is a good point, that it is indeed remarkable that so high a level of fees can be charged for apparently so little result, turns out to be a point of little if any substance. I am not prepared to regard it as amounting to a special circumstance justifying assessment of those bills".*

5.44. The judge also made the point that it would *"be surprising if relatively minor queries about items in the bill could amount to special circumstances."*

Where a Client is dissuaded from seeking an assessment

5.45. In *Kralj v Birckbeck Montague*[19] the solicitors had charged a significant amount more than the client recovered between the parties and had put pressure on her not to have the solicitor client costs assessed. The court found that this amounted to special circumstances.

Advice as to Assessment wrong

5.46. Beatson J considered circumstances in *Kundruth v Henry Kwatia & Gooding*[20] where the solicitor had erroneously advised the client:

---

17 (1867) LR 3 Ex 4

18 [2000] BCC 310

19 Unreported. [1988] Lexis Citation 1796

20 [2004] EWHC 2852 (QB)

"It is a matter for you to apply to the Supreme Court Costs Office for an order that this bill be assessed. Since more than one month has elapsed any order made by the court to assess the bill will be conditional on you paying into court 40% of the bill." [3]

5.47. The judge held that:

"I have concluded that...the letter was not merely "inaccurate" and "a misrepresentation" but, given the inequality of the parties, it amounted to the sort of pressure which it has been recognised is capable of amounting to special circumstances" [11]

Agreement between solicitor and client to assess

5.48. An agreement to have an assessment will ordinarily amount to special circumstances. Per Briggs QC in *Arrowfield Services Limited v B P Collins (a firm)[21]*:

"... if parties come before the court on an application for a detailed assessment in circumstances where there subsists an agreement that there should be such an assessment to which the solicitor has consented, and from which he has not freed himself in the manner which I have described, or in some other recognisable manner, that is as powerful a special circumstance as it is possible to conceive for ordering a detailed assessment". [38]

Payment with reservation of right to assess

5.49. If a client explicitly states that he wishes to have the costs assessed when paying the bill this can amount to special circumstances.[22]

5.50. However, the mere fact that a client has reserved their rights to have the bill assessed is not determinative. Per Holroyde J (in refusing an appeal from a costs judge who held that there were no special circumstances despite the reservation of the right to assess by the client):

---

21 [2003] EWHC 830 (Ch) at [9]

22 Solicitors, Re (1934) 50 TLR 327 and also see Sanders & Anor v. Isaacs & Anor - [1971] 1 WLR 240 at pg 247

"...it is important to bear in mind that in a situation such as this the court is being asked to exercise a discretion which only arises if special circumstances are shown, and it is therefore necessary to have regard to all the circumstances of the particular case. I accept that a reservation of the right to tax is a highly important factor, but it is not to be viewed in isolation". [107]

Solicitor refusing to provide details or a breakdown

5.51. Pumfrey J held in *Re Metal Distributors Ltd* [23] that the mere fact that the solicitors had refused to provide a breakdown of the bill did not amount to special circumstances:

"The company...urges upon me the consideration that the company has reasonably asked the solicitors for a breakdown of the bill which has been declined. Whether that is a matter of good client management or not is not a matter for me, since I am concerned only with the question whether these bills are presently payable. In my judgment they plainly are. It is accepted that there is no challenge to the quality of the work done by Messrs Devonshires which is represented by the bills, and there is no suggestion of any claim in respect of negligence". [3-4]

5.52. What the client should have done in those circumstances was to begin the assessment process in time and seek a direction for a breakdown of the bill (which would have been made as a matter of course by the court).

Prejudice

5.53. Where the solicitor can show that a delay in seeking assessment has caused prejudice this will be relevant. Conversely, where there is no evidence that the delay caused *"significant prejudice"* [24] it is unlikely to be taken into account.

---

23 [2004] EWHC 2535 (Ch)

24 Kundruth v Henry Kwatia & Gooding [2004] EWHC 2852 (QB) at [15]

Who May Apply For an Assessment? Third Parties

As if they were the client: s.71(1)

5.54. It is obvious that the client may apply for an assessment of their solicitor's costs but there are a number of other parties who may have an interest in the fees claimed but who are not strictly the solicitor's client.

5.55. The Act at s.71 provides that third parties can apply for an assessment where they are liable to pay the bill despite not being the party chargeable:

> "Where a person other than the party chargeable with the bill for the purposes of section 70 has paid, or is or was liable to pay, a bill either to the solicitor or to the party chargeable with the bill, that person, or his executors, administrators or assignees may apply to the High Court for an order for the assessment of the bill as if he were the party chargeable with it, and the court may make the same order (if any) as it might have made if the application had been made by the party chargeable with the bill."

5.56. There are numerous examples of third parties who could apply for an assessment under s.71(1). The following list is not exhaustive:

(i) A third party who undertakes to pay costs as between solicitor and client as a term of compromise or settlement.

(ii) The liquidator of a company

(iii) A mortgagee or the trustee in bankruptcy of a mortgagee

(iv) A lessee who under a contract must pay his landlord's costs

5.57. Where the third party makes an application under s.71 the court will essentially treat them as though they were the party chargeable. Per s.71(2) if the court is required to consider special circumstances it may take into account circumstances which affect the applicant but do not affect the party chargeable with the bill.

5.58. As the third party is treated as though they were the party chargeable the court is only able to make the orders they could have made <u>had the party chargeable applied</u>. Thus, the time limits and strict bar to an assessment post twelve months after payment apply.

5.59. In *Tim Martin Interiors v Akin Gump*[25] the court of appeal considered the limitations of an assessment under s.71(1). In that case the claimant had borrowed money from a bank with the loan secured by way of a mortgage. The claimant defaulted on the mortgage.

5.60. The mortgage deed contained a clause which required them to pay the bank's costs of enforcing its security and the bank instructed Akin Gump solicitors. Their fees totalled £123,000 and were paid when the bank transferred the mortgage to two directors of the claimant in consideration for the payment of the outstanding sums.

5.61. The claimant then sought an assessment of Akin Gump's fees and brought an application for assessment against them under s.71. Having exhaustively gone through the rules and applicable case law Lloyd LJ concluded:

> "...a third party assessment under section 71 is of limited use to a third party. As regards quantification it only allows the costs judge to follow what might be called a blue pencil approach. He can eliminate (a) items which ought not to be laid at the door of the third party at all because they are outwith the scope of his liability, here as mortgagor, and (b) items which are only allowable as between client and solicitor on a special arrangement basis, within the terms of CPR rule 48.8(2)(c). He cannot either eliminate any other item or reduce the quantum of any item which is properly included in itself, but for which he considers that the charge made is excessive, unless he could have done so as between client and solicitor on an assessment under section 70." [95]

5.62. An example is the hourly rate. In an assessment under s.71(1) the court may only interfere with an hourly rate if it could have done so on a solicitor and client basis. In the *Tim Martin* case the claimant argued that a City of London firm should not have been instructed. This is not an argument that a client could bring against his solicitor (for the obvi-

---

25 [2011] EWCA Civ 1574

ous reason that he chose to instruct that particular firm!) That is not the sort of point that can be taken in a s.71(1) assessment.

5.63. Further, the court found that where a third party has paid the fees to the client, who then pays the solicitor, then even if the court reduced the bill on assessment *"it is not open to the court to require the solicitor to refund the balance to the third party. The liability to repay lies with the client, not with the solicitor."* [94]

5.64. Lloyd LJ gave this advice to mortgagees seeking an assessment as third parties[26]:

> *"...the third party ought to bring proceedings against the client to establish how much was due from him to the client. In a mortgage case such as the present, the proceedings would be conventional proceedings for an account of what was due under the mortgage. Such proceedings would enable the court to determine the correct issue as between the correct parties, and if appropriate to order repayment by the mortgagee to the mortgagor. In such proceedings it would be possible for the court to do what cannot be done under a section 71 assessment, namely to disallow part of an amount claimed on the basis that something was due, but not as much as is claimed – for example by substituting a lower hourly rate."* [98]

Trustees, Executors and Administrators: s.71(3)

5.65. The Act at s.71(3) and (4) deals with the position where trustees, executors or administrators become liable to pay a solicitor's bill. In that circumstance any person with an interest in the property out of which the bill has been or will be paid is able to apply to have the bill assessed.

5.66. The court, when considering such an application will take into account the extent and nature of the interest of the applicant (s.71(3)(4) (b)). The wording is as follows:

> *"Where a trustee, executor or administrator has become liable to pay a bill of a solicitor, then, on the application of any person interested in any property out of which the trustee, executor or administrator has paid, or is entitled to pay, the bill, the court may order—*

---

26 For the procedure involved see [100] of the judgment.

(a) that the bill be assessed on such terms, if any, as it thinks fit; and

(b) that such payments, in respect of the amount found to be due to or by the solicitor and in respect of the costs of the assessment, be made to or by the applicant, to or by the solicitor, or to or by the executor, administrator or trustee, as it thinks fit.

(4) In considering any application under subsection (3) the court shall have regard—

(a) to the provisions of section 70 as to applications by the party chargeable for the assessment of a solicitor's bill so far as they are capable of being applied to an application made under that subsection;

(b) to the extent and nature of the interest of the applicant."

5.67. In *McIlwraith v McIlwraith*[27] HHJ Rich QC sitting as a High Court Judge held that the strict time limits under s.70 of the Act do not apply to applications under s.71(3). So, for example, the court has a discretion to allow an assessment more than twelve months after the bill has been paid.

5.68. The judgment in *Tim Martin* (above) appears to include both s.71(1) and 71(3) in its scope. It is not clear whether the distinction between the two sections was ever brought to the court's attention.

5.69. It is arguable however that applications under s.71(3) are made on a different basis and <u>not</u> as though the applicant was 'the party chargeable'.

5.70. If that is right, then there should be no issue with the beneficiary seeking an assessment under the Act and being able to challenge items (without being curtailed by the *Tim Martin* restrictions).

5.71. The problem is that it is arguable that s.71(3) is a subordinate part of s.71 generally and as a result the guidance at s.71(1) applies to that class of party as well as to those who stand in the shoes of the client.

---

27 [2002] EWHC 1757 (Ch)

5.72. This is an important point for beneficiaries who wish to challenge the costs incurred by solicitors (for example, the costs incurred in relation to the administration of an estate). If they are curtailed by the restrictions of s.71(1) then they will be unable to properly challenge any bill save as far as *Tim Martin* allows[28].

5.73. This is problematic because, per *Tim Martin*, to circumvent the restrictions on the ability to challenge the costs, the beneficiary must bring an action for an account. That is a discretionary power but the court would be likely to order an account where there were clear and justifiable reasons (for example, where the beneficiary could show, prima facie, that the costs charged are wholly unreasonable).

5.74. The hurdles do not end there. If an account is ordered the next question is what can be challenged? In *Mussell & Anor v Patience & Anor*[29] the court found that:

> *"On the taking of an account, the executor will be entitled to all "just allowances"…What are "just allowances"? They are… "whatever a trustee or representative has expended in the fair execution of his trust". In my judgment, whatever the position on detailed assessment of costs, in relation to accounting to his or her beneficiaries for what has been done with the estate, an executor has only to show (1) that the sum concerned was indeed spent, and (2) that it was spent in the fair execution of the estate administration."* [14]

5.75. In respect of how the executor can show that the sum was spent and spent in fair execution of the estate administration, the judge said:

---

28 The potential issues here are obvious. Solicitors who are executors regularly instruct their own firms to undertake the work, meaning that if a trustee or beneficiary can only 'stand in the shoes of the client', the 'client' would be the solicitor! All the solicitor would need to do is show that they gave instructions to their own firm and agreed the costs for any potential challenge to be lost.

29 [2018] EWHC 430 (Ch). The judge in this case was seemingly not referred to *Tim Martin* and the court of appeal's view that an account was the appropriate mechanism by which the unjust consequences of a s.71(1) assessment could be avoided. It is arguable that the decision in *Mussell* was given per incuriam and was wrongly decided (or would have been decided differently had the judge considered the *Tim Martin* judgment).

"The former will normally be demonstrated by a document ("the voucher") showing payment or receipt. The latter will normally be demonstrated by a document such as an invoice referring to the executor as such, to administration of the estate or to some good or service having a connection with the estate (eg repairs to estate property). It will of course be open to the beneficiaries to rebut the inference in either case, but unless and until some other evidence is adduced by the beneficiaries to that end, the executor in my judgment need do nothing more." [15]

5.76. As a result, if the executor can show payment or receipt and then an invoice setting out what was done, then prima facie, the court approves the amount.

5.77. The *Mussell* judgment makes the point that taking an account is not the same as a detailed assessment. So, the beneficiary can seek an assessment under the Act but is back in the *Tim Martin* situation, with all the resulting restrictions on challenges!

5.78. The law is not settled on this point. It is wholly unsatisfactory[30] that third parties under s.71(3) have no clarity as to their rights to challenge what they consider excessive costs however, in the absence of a decision of authority which clarifies the point, or a statutory change, the uncertainty will continue.

---

30 The Senior Costs Judge Master Gordon-Saker raised the issue at a Civil Justice Council event in June 2018 when suggesting a review of the Act saying "We could…have addressed the position of third parties who are liable to pay bills but have effectively lost their right to challenge those bills following the decision in *Tim Martin v Akin Gump.*"

CHAPTER SIX
PROCEDURE

Introduction

6.1. As discussed in Chapter Five, save for the exceptions listed, a solicitor must wait for at least one month after delivery of a statute bill before commencing proceedings to recover their fees.

6.2. If the client has already made an application to have the bill assessed before the proceedings are issued then the court will order that no proceedings are commenced in respect of the bill. Thus, if the client has already sought assessment the solicitor may not sue on the bill (and it would be pointless to do so).

6.3. It is often the case that the client issues an application for assessment after the solicitor has issued proceedings for recovery of their fees. Where this occurs, the court will order that the recovery proceedings are not continued with while the assessment is ongoing.

6.4. The Limitation Act 1980 applies to solicitor and client retainers. The time begins running from the date upon which the cause of action arises; that is, the date when the solicitors become entitled to their fees.

6.5. The application for an order for assessment must be made using the Part 8 procedure save where it is made in existing proceedings (CPR r.67(2)). Costs Precedent J (to PD47.30) is a model claim form for use when seeking an assessment under the Act.

6.6. If the bill is less than £5,000 and the matter relates wholly or partly to contentious business done in the county court then per s.69(3) of the Act the application for assessment may be made in the county court. Even where the value is modest it is worth considering whether a specialist costs judge in the SCCO would be better suited to considering the issues than a district judge in the county court (who may never have dealt with a solicitor client action before).

6.7. Per CPR 67.3(1) where the bill is does not comply with the criteria above, the application for an order for assessment must be made in the

High Court. If the Part 8 claim is issued in the High Court in London it must be issued within the SCCO.[1] In any other case it may be issued in the SCCO.[2]

6.8. Where a solicitor has brought Part 7 proceedings for recovery of his fees in the High Court and the liability for fees is not in dispute (but the quantum is) then the client should apply for an order that the matter be referred to a costs judge for assessment. CPR r.67.3(2) states that such an application must be made formally in accordance with Part 23 CPR.

6.9. On the other hand, if the client is denying that they owe the fees at all (because, for example, they argue that the retainer was terminated unlawfully) then this can be considered as a preliminary issue. Only if the client was held liable for the fees would the matter need to be referred to a costs judge.[3]

6.10. In *Badaei v Woodward Solicitors*[4] there was an issue between the client and solicitor as to whether the CFA had been terminated lawfully. The client issued Part 8 assessment proceedings under the Act and the solicitor subsequently issued Part 7 debt recovery /breach of contract proceedings.

6.11. At first instance the judge struck out the Part 8 claim on the basis that the case was not suitable for Part 8. On appeal O'Farrell J overturned this decision and found that:

> "Part 8 proceedings generally are not suitable to determine serious disputes of fact…I also accept that on the current pleadings, although it is dealt with by way of a bare denial in the defence, there is a dispute as to whether or not, both factually and legally, the appellant is in breach of the CFA and whether or not that would have any consequences regarding the respondent's ability to recover their fees

---

1 PD67.2.1(1) CPR

2 PD67.2.1(2) CPR

3 In practice the court may consider that a costs judge, rather than a High Court judge would be best placed to consider both the preliminary issue and the further objections and refer the entirety of the dispute to the SCCO at the outset.

4 [2019] Costs LR 1253

and disbursements....However, on balance, I consider that that could be accommodated fairly readily within the Part 8 proceedings." [58-60]

6.12. As a result, all the issues were considered within the Part 8 assessment proceedings.

6.13. The PD47 at 6.4 sets out what must be included with an application for an order under Part III of the Act[5]:

"The application must be accompanied by the bill or bills in respect of which assessment is sought, and, if the claim concerns a conditional fee agreement, a copy of that agreement. If the original bill is not available a copy will suffice."

6.14. It should be noted that there are no default judgment provisions under Part 8 as the provisions of Part 15 CPR do not apply.[6] Thus, if the defendant does not respond to the claim form the claimant will not be able to request summary judgment. Rather, if the defendant does not file an acknowledgment of service within 14 days of service of the claim form they will not be able to take part in the hearing (but may attend) unless the court gives permission.[7]

6.15. The court will then list a directions hearing. If there are preliminary issues to decide first then these will be listed for hearing, along with evidence to be filed in support of the submissions of the parties. For example, if special circumstances are required then the court will consider this first- for the obvious reason that if the client's argument fails there will be no right to an assessment at all.

6.16. If, however, the parties agree that there should be an assessment or the court has already determined that the client has such a right the standard directions at CPR r.46.10 will be issued:

---

5 Part III of the Act begins at s.56 and includes the rules relating to the remuneration of solicitors. The earlier parts of the Act deal with the practice rules and disciplinary provisions relating to solicitors. All assessment of costs under the Act will be under Part III.

6 CPR PD8A 5.1

7 CPR r.8.4(2)

"(1) This rule sets out the procedure to be followed where the court has made an order under Part III of the Solicitors Act 1974 for the assessment of costs payable to a solicitor by the solicitor's client.

(2) The solicitor must serve a breakdown of costs within 28 days of the order for costs to be assessed.

(3) The client must serve points of dispute within 14 days after service on the client of the breakdown of costs.

(4) The solicitor must serve any reply within 14 days of service on the solicitor of the points of dispute.

(5) Either party may file a request for a hearing date –

(a) after points of dispute have been served; but

(b) no later than 3 months after the date of the order for the costs to be assessed.

(6) This procedure applies subject to any contrary order made by the court."

6.17. The PD46.6.6 CPR states that the breakdown of costs referred to above must include:

"(a) details of the work done under each of the bills sent for assessment; and

(b) in applications under Section 70 of the Solicitors Act 1974, a cash account showing money received by the solicitor to the credit of the client and sums paid out of that money on behalf of the client but not payments out which were made in satisfaction of the bill or of any items which are claimed in the bill."

6.18. A cash account sets out the payments and receipts made on behalf of the client and includes items that are not properly included within the bill as disbursements but charged in the cash account. Examples are damages, costs paid to the opponent and interest.

6.19. The PD46.6.7 also requires that the following is served with a breakdown:

> *"(a) copies of the fee notes of counsel and of any expert in respect of fees claimed in the breakdown, and*
>
> *(b) written evidence as to any other disbursement which is claimed in the breakdown and which exceeds £250."*

6.20. It is important to note that the statute bill is the bill assessed, not the breakdown. The breakdown will assist the court in assessing the bill but does not supersede it[8]; the figure for the purposes of the one fifth rule (see below) is the amount of the bill.

6.21. A precedent breakdown of costs in a solicitor client assessment is at Costs Precedent P (PD47.33). If the bill is sufficiently detailed the court need not order a breakdown to be prepared.

Points of dispute and replies

6.22. Points of dispute and replies will follow the format of those served in between the parties dispute. There is a precedent points of dispute and reply at PD47.27 (Precedent G).

6.23. *Ainsworth v Stewart Law LLP*[9] is a salutary lesson for clients in respect of the required format of points of dispute. In that case the client drafted generic and undetailed objections to the document time claimed by the solicitor (which comprised the majority of the fees claimed).

6.24. The solicitor objected to the points of dispute and sought greater detail. The client failed to clarify the basis of their objections.

6.25. At first instance the senior costs judge dismissed the objections to the document time and allowed the fees in full.

---

8   See Re: Tilleard 32 Beav. 476

9   [2019] EWCA Civ 897

6.26. The Court of Appeal upheld this decision. Asplin LJ gave guidance as to the how points of dispute should be drafted in solicitor and client assessments:

> *"Common sense dictates that the points of dispute must be drafted in a way which enables the parties and the court to determine precisely what is in dispute and why. That is the very purposes of such a document. It is necessary in order to enable the receiving party, the solicitor in this case, to be able to reply to the complaints. It is also necessary in order to enable the court to deal with the issues raised in a manner which is fair, just and proportionate."* [38]

6.27. The judge went on to say:

> *"In the case of a solicitor and own client assessment, it seems to me, therefore, that in order to specify the nature and grounds of the dispute it is necessary to formulate specific points by reference to the presumptions contained CPR 46.9(3) which would otherwise apply, to specify the specific items in the bill to which they relate and to make clear in each case why the item is disputed. This need not be a lengthy process."* [39]

6.28. As can be seen, drafting points of dispute in solicitor and client assessments is not identical to between the parties cases. There must be a focus on the presumptions at r.46.9(3)[10] and the objections must allow the solicitor to (a) properly understand why the client argues that the fees are unreasonable and (b) attempt to justify the costs claimed.

6.29. This case shows the dire consequences for a client who fails to draft points of dispute correctly.

6.30. The rules relating to default costs certificates do not apply to solicitor and client assessments (PD46.6.8).

6.31. However, if a party fails to comply with the directions and does not serve a breakdown of costs, points of dispute or replies in the time set by the court the other party may seek an unless order which sets out the sanction for failure to comply (PD46. 6.3). If a breakdown or replies are not served the client should seek an unless order which

---

10 See "Basis of Assessment" below.

strikes out the costs if the default is not rectified within a reasonable time. If the client has not served points of dispute the solicitor should seek an order that they are debarred from taking part in the assessment unless the points are served within a reasonable time.

Requesting a hearing

6.32. When requesting a hearing Form N258C must be used (PD46.6.10). The following documents must be sent with the form:

(a) the order sending the bill or bills for assessment;

(b) the bill or bills sent for assessment;

(c) the solicitor's breakdown of costs and any invoices or accounts served with that breakdown;

(d) a copy of the points of dispute;

(e) a copy of any replies served;

(f) a statement signed by the party filing the request or that party's legal representative giving the names and addresses for service of all parties to the proceedings;

6.33. The request must include the estimated length of hearing.

Delivery Up of Documents

6.34. If the client wishes to assess his solicitor's bill she (or those who advise her) will require sight of the documents produced during the retainer. These would include letters to him and letters to and from third parties.

6.35. If the client does not have the documents he can seek delivery up under s.68 of the Act. This provides:

"(1) The jurisdiction of the High Court to make orders for the delivery by a solicitor of a bill of costs, and for the delivery up of, or otherwise in relation to, any documents in his possession, custody or power,

is hereby declared to extend to cases in which no business has been done by him in the High Court.

(2) The county court and the family court each have the same jurisdiction as the High Court to make orders making such provision as is mentioned in subsection (1) in cases where the bill of costs or the documents relate wholly or partly to contentious business done by the solicitor in the county court or (as the case may be) the family court."

6.36. Documents can be put into the following categories; those that belong to the client and those over which the solicitor has a proprietary right.

6.37. Documents belonging to the <u>client</u> will include:

(i) Documents created by third parties and paid for by the client (for example, counsel's advice)

(ii) Documents sent to or received from third parties

(iii) Documents sent to the solicitors by the client

6.38. Documents which belong to the <u>solicitor</u> include:

(i) Internal correspondence

(ii) Letters/emails to the firm from the client

(iii) Accounting records

(iv) Copies of letters sent to the client

(v) Other documents prepared for the solicitor's own benefit (e.g. notes taken of advice given)

6.39. It is uncontroversial that the client is entitled to copies of those documents that belong to them (although the solicitor may charge for producing copies)[11].

---

11 In re Thomson - (1855) 52 ER 714 which provides that "On payment of a solicitor's bill, the client is entitled to the possession of letters written to the solicitor

6.40. However, Soole J in *Hanley v JCA Solicitors*[12] held that the court has no power to order disclosure of copies of documents which are the property of the solicitor, for three reasons:

"First, as a matter of principle, an order for delivery up or otherwise in relation to property belonging to another must have an explicit legal basis.

Secondly, the powers referred to in s.68 are derived from the inherent jurisdiction, not the statute itself. The section simply extends the reach of the jurisdiction to cases in which no business has been done in the High Court. It reflects, with immaterial amendments, the provisions of successive statutes governing solicitors. Thus the scope of the jurisdiction is to be identified from authority, rather than interpretation of the statutory language.

Thirdly, the decisions relied on by the appellants in my judgment provide no authority for their central proposition that the Court has a discretion under the inherent jurisdiction to order delivery up or make other orders in respect of documents which belong to the solicitor." [61-63]

6.41. As a result, where a client requests copies of documents belonging to the solicitor, they can refuse to provide them. This is an important right in theory, because the context of such a request is almost always as a precursor to considering whether to have an assessment of the solicitor's fees.

6.42. Soole J did however sound a warning to solicitors not to unreasonably refuse such a request:

"All that said, it does not follow that solicitors should in all circumstances press their legal rights to the limit, nor that they can necessarily do so with impunity. To take one example, a refusal to comply with a former client's request for a copy of a mislaid CFA (made on an undertaking to pay a reasonable copying charge) so that advice

by third parties, but not to copies of letters written by the solicitor to third parties, unless they are paid for by the client."

12 Full title: Hanley v JCA Solicitors, Green & Ors v SGI Legal LLP [2018] EWHC 2592 (QB).

may be obtained on the prospects of a s.70 application, would surely entitle the client to issue such an application notwithstanding the inability to comply with the procedural requirement in PD46 para. 6.4; and could have potential adverse costs implications for the solicitors within those proceedings, whatever their result." [74]

6.43. Each case will turn on its facts but broadly, if the document is one that the client has already received (and perhaps misplaced) and there is likely to be an assessment in any event, no great advantage is to be gained from a refusal to disclose. It should be noted that, upon an assessment being granted, the client will have the right to inspect the *entirety* of the solicitors' files and therefore a refusal to send a document to them may simply cause expense and delay (which could sound in costs against the solicitor if their conduct is deemed unreasonable).

The Assessment

6.44. The court will not necessarily assess every part of the bill. It is open to the client or party chargeable to seek an assessment of a discrete element.

6.45. The Act at s.70(5) and (6) provides that:

"(5) An order for the assessment of a bill made on an application under this section by the party chargeable with the bill shall, if he so requests, be an order for the assessment of the profit costs covered by the bill.

(6) Subject to subsection (5), the court may under this section order the assessment of all the costs, or of the profit costs, or of the costs other than profit costs and, where part of the costs is not to be assessed, may allow an action to be commenced or to be continued for that part of the costs."

6.46. This enables the client to assess only the part of a bill which is considered unreasonable. For example, the client may consider that disbursements are perfectly reasonable but object to the level of profit costs. In that instance they would seek assessment of the profit costs only. This has very important implications in relation to the one fifth rule (see below).

6.47. It should be noted that where the client does not seek an assessment of part of the bill, the solicitor may sue for payment of the uncontentious element (or may continue with an action for those costs alone).

6.48. It is not unusual in solicitor and client assessments to hear live evidence. This is particularly so where there is a point of principle in dispute (for example, which party terminated the retainer or where there is a dispute about reliance on estimates).

6.49. A party who wishes to put in a witness statement as evidence should ensure that they obtain suitable directions at the initial hearing. The court can also provide permission for cross examination (which will avoid the party having to make an application under CPR r.32.7).

Attendance at the Assessment

6.50. Any lawyer with a right of audience under the Legal Services Act 2007 may attend the assessment as an advocate. That includes counsel, solicitors and costs lawyers. Legal Executives in the employ of solicitors (or those with the advocacy qualification obtained from CILEX) may also appear.

6.51. Litigants in person may appear at the assessment on their own behalf. A bankrupt may not be heard save in limited circumstances.[13]

6.52. The officers or employees of a company may only be heard with the court's permission (although the PD39A.5.3 makes it clear that the court should ordinarily grant such permission.) However, the company should seek such permission in advance of the hearing.

6.53. Costs draftsmen who are not costs lawyers do not have a freestanding right of audience in assessment proceedings, however, where they are employed by a solicitor they are heard as unqualified persons who appear under the instruction and supervision of a solicitor.

6.54. Independent costs draftsmen who are not costs lawyers are heard in the SCCO, by concession, as though they were in the employ of the qualified lawyer who has instructed them.[14] They may not represent litigants in person.

---

13 See for example, s.303 of the Insolvency Act 1986

6.55. A 'Mackenzie friend' can assist a litigant in person in court but may not address the court save with the court's permission. The ability of a Mackenzie Friend to recover costs is severely restricted.[15]

6.56. The Act at s.70(8) provides that where a party fails to attend the hearing, having been given notice of the assessment, the court may (at its discretion) proceed with the hearing ex parte[16].

The Basis of Assessment[17]

6.57. The biggest difference between the basis of a solicitor and client assessment and a between the parties assessment is that in the later the court will take into account proportionality when considering the costs. Proportionality is excluded from solicitor client assessments and plays no part in the court determining whether costs will be allowed, disallowed or reduced.

6.58. The costs will be assessed on the indemnity basis but this is not the same as the indemnity basis between the parties. Rather, the assessment proceeds on a number of presumptions (which are rebuttable[18]) set out within CPR r. 46.9(3):

> *"costs are to be assessed on the indemnity basis but are to be presumed*
> —
>
> *(a) to have been reasonably incurred if they were incurred with the express or implied approval of the client;*
>
> *(b) to be reasonable in amount if their amount was expressly or impliedly approved by the client;*
>
> *(c) to have been unreasonably incurred if –*

14 See the SCCO Guide 2013 at 1.2(d)

15 See Practice Guidance (Mackenzie Friends : Civil and Family Courts) [2010] 1 W.L.R. 1881

16 Namely, without hearing from the party who does not attend.

17 This section is not concerned with the assessment of contentious or non-contentious business agreements which are dealt with in Chapter One

18 PD46.6.2

(i) they are of an unusual nature or amount; and

(ii) the solicitor did not tell the client that as a result the costs might not be recovered from the other party."

6.59. The PD46.6.1 explains:

"A client and solicitor may agree whatever terms they consider appropriate about the payment of the solicitor's charges. If however, the costs are of an unusual nature, either in amount or the type of costs incurred, those costs will be presumed to have been unreasonably incurred unless the solicitor satisfies the court that the client was informed that they were unusual and that they might not be allowed on an assessment of costs between the parties. That information must have been given to the client before the costs were incurred."

6.60. Thus, if a client can show that an item or class or items within the bill are (a) of an unusual nature and (b) the client was not told (before the costs were incurred) that they were unusual and might not be allowed between the parties there will be a presumption that they have been unreasonably incurred.

6.61. In *Mac-Dougall v Boote Edgar Esterkin*[19] Holland J considered a situation where the client had agreed an hourly rate with his solicitor of £300 (which in 2001 was unusually high). The issue was whether the presumption at r.46.9(3) CPR[20] applied and the rate should be presumed to be reasonable because it had been set with the approval of the client.

6.62. Holland J found that it should not, stating:

"To rely on the Applicants' approval the solicitor must satisfy me that it was secured following a full and fair exposition of the factors relevant to it so that the Applicants, lay persons as they are, can reasonably be bound by it." [8]

---

19 [2001] 1 Costs LR 118

20 In fact, the court considered Order 62 r. 15(2) as this was a pre-CPR case, however, those provisions mirror r.44.6.9(3)

6.63. In *Herbert v HH Law*[21], the Court of Appeal clarified which party has the burden of proving that informed consent was given:

> *"We consider that where, as here, the client brings proceedings under the Solicitors Act 1974 s.70(1), it is for the client to state the point of dispute and the grounds for it. If the solicitor wishes to rebut the challenge by relying on the presumption in CPR 46.9(3)(a) or (b), the burden lies on the solicitor to show that the pre-condition of the presumption, informed approval, is satisfied.*
>
> *Once the solicitor has adduced evidence to show that the client gave informed consent, the evidential burden will move to the client to show why, as a result of having been given insufficiently clear or accurate or comprehensive information by the solicitor or for some other reason, there was no consent or it was not informed consent.*
>
> *The overall burden of showing that informed consent was given remains on the solicitor."* [38]

6.64. In *Breyer Group PLC & Ors v Prospect Law Ltd*[22] Master Rowley considered whether charging a client in 10-minute units, rather than the more usual 6 minute units, was 'unusual' despite the client agreeing to such charging within the retainer. He found that:

> *"The invariable practice is for bills to claim routine items at 6 minutes... Given that this is an uncommon practice, it seems to me that the express agreement of the claimants to the terms of the client care letter is not the end of the matter. The claimants needed to be told that routine items claimed at 10 minutes were unlikely to be recovered on that basis. Whilst a routine letter could hardly be described as being unusual in nature, it seems to me that charging a 10 minute unit for such a communication could quite properly be described as being unusual in nature. It is beyond doubt that it is unusual in amount."* [20-21]

6.65. Thus, despite the agreement of the client within the retainer letter, the judge held that the explanation given was inadequate. The soli-

---

21 [2019] EWCA Civ 527

22 Unreported. SCCO 26/7/17. The judgment is widely available online.

citor had told the clients that the they would likely recover 70% of their costs between the parties at a detailed assessment but that was a general point and did not specifically state that, even for the 70%, the <u>recoverable</u> letters would be reduced from 10 minutes to 6 minutes.

6.56. The judge also found that it would be unreasonable for the clients to be charged the full rate for incoming correspondence as this would be unusual (but the mere fact that incoming letters were not recoverable on a between the parties basis did not mean that they were unusual items on a solicitor and client basis). A charge of half the 6-minute unit rate was allowed. [41]-[42].

6.67. The question of whether a charge is unusual in nature or amount will be fact specific and is ultimately a matter of discretion. Costs judges are well placed to consider whether an item is unusual using their experience of assessing bills. If solicitors wish to claim costs from their client which could be considered unusual they must ensure that the client is told specifically that the item is unusual and that they will may not recover the costs from the opposing party.

6.68. Ultimately, any approval by the client must be on the basis of a full and fair explanation.

<u>Contentious costs</u>

6.69. Contentious costs will be assessed with reference to CPR r.44.4 which sets out the factors to be taken into account:

"(1) The court will have regard to all the circumstances in deciding whether costs were –

(a) if it is assessing costs on the standard basis –

(i) proportionately and reasonably incurred; or

(ii) proportionate and reasonable in amount, or

(b) if it is assessing costs on the indemnity basis –

(i) unreasonably incurred; or

(ii) unreasonable in amount.

(2) In particular, the court will give effect to any orders which have already been made.

(3) The court will also have regard to –

(a) the conduct of all the parties, including in particular –

(i) conduct before, as well as during, the proceedings; and

(ii) the efforts made, if any, before and during the proceedings in order to try to resolve the dispute;

(b) the amount or value of any money or property involved;

(c) the importance of the matter to all the parties;

(d) the particular complexity of the matter or the difficulty or novelty of the questions raised;

(e) the skill, effort, specialised knowledge and responsibility involved;

(f) the time spent on the case;

(g) the place where and the circumstances in which work or any part of it was done; and

(h) the receiving party's last approved or agreed budget."

Non-contentious costs

6.70. The CPR r.44.3(6) provides that:

"Where the amount of a solicitor's remuneration in respect of non-contentious business is regulated by any general orders made under the Solicitors Act 1974, the amount of the costs to be allowed in respect of any such business which falls to be assessed by the court will be decided in accordance with those general orders rather than this rule and rule 44.4"

6.71. As a result, the factors set out above do not apply. Rather, the costs will be assessed with reference to the factors set out in The Solicitors' (Non-Contentious Business) Remuneration Order 2009 article 3:

"A solicitor's costs must be fair and reasonable having regard to all the circumstances of the case and in particular to—

(a) the complexity of the matter or the difficulty or novelty of the questions raised;

(b) the skill, labour, specialised knowledge and responsibility involved;

(c) the time spent on the business;

(d) the number and importance of the documents prepared or considered, without regard to length;

(e) the place where and the circumstances in which the business or any part of the business is transacted;

(f) the amount or value of any money or property involved;

(g) whether any land involved is registered land within the meaning of the Land Registration Act 2002;

(h) the importance of the matter to the client; and

(i) the approval (express or implied) of the entitled person or the express approval of the testator to—

(i) the solicitor undertaking all or any part of the work giving rise to the costs; or

(ii) the amount of the costs."

6.72. In probate matters a solicitor may charge a 'value element' based on the value of the estate. The value element must be fair and reasonable per article 3 above.

6.73. The value element was considered in *Jemma Trust Co Ltd v Liptrott*.[23] The court found that it was still permissible to charge a value element in addition to hourly rate charges but it cannot be included in both:

> "...there should be no hard and fast rule that charges cannot be made separately by reference to the value of the estate; value can, by contrast, be taken into account as part of the hourly rate; value can also be taken into account partly in one way and partly in the other. What is important is that
>
> (a) it should be transparent on the face of the bill how value is being taken into account; and
>
> (b) in no case, should it be taken into account more than once" [33]

6.74. As a point of general principle Longmore LJ said that it was:

> "...apparent that the amount or value of any money or property involved in the estate being administered is a matter to which regard is to be had in assessing the fair and reasonable remuneration to which solicitors are entitled." [3]

6.75. Longmore LJ gave the following guidance in relation to different size estates:

> "In an estate of small or medium-value, it may be appropriate for a solicitor to limit his charges to a percentage of the estate's value or to charge a percentage together with an appropriately modest hourly rate. For a high-value estate it may also be appropriate to charge a percentage together with an hourly rate because, if one is to take value into account, as the Order entitles the solicitor and requires the costs judge to do, that will mean that the charges will have one element of comparative certainty." [24]

6.76. As guidance for costs judges, the court said:

---

23 [2003] EWCA Civ 1476

"We would, however, say that it will usually be right to reduce the value element percentage by reference to a regressive scale in some such way as was done by Walton J in Maltby v DJ Freeman." [29]

6.77. It was suggested at [30] that, for work undertaken in 2003, the following scale would be appropriate:

Up to £1m	1.5 %
£1m – £4m	1/2 %
£4m – £8m	1/6 %
£8m – 12m	1/12 %

6.78. However, in giving this guidance Longmore LJ made it clear that the ultimate decision was a matter for the costs judge's discretion:

"...in many cases, if a charge is separately made by reference to the value of the estate, it should usually be on a regressive scale. The bands and percentages will be for the costs judge in each case; the suggestions to the costs judge set out in paragraph 30 may be thought by him to be appropriate for this case but different bands and percentages will be appropriate for other cases and the figures set out in paragraph 30 cannot be any more than a guideline" [33]

6.79. Ultimately, the costs judge must consider whether the costs claimed, including the value charge are fair and reasonable.

The Costs of the Assessment

6.80. The Act provides clear guidance on which party will pay the costs of a solicitor and client assessment at s.70(9):

"Unless—

(a) the order for assessment was made on the application of the solicitor and the party chargeable does not attend the assessment, or

*(b) the order for assessment or an order under subsection (10) other-
wise provides, the costs of an assessment shall be paid according to the
event of the assessment, that is to say, if the amount of the bill is reduced by one fifth, the solicitor shall pay the costs, but otherwise the
party chargeable shall pay the costs."*

6.81. At s.70(10) the Act states:

*"The costs officer may certify to the court any special circumstances re-
lating to a bill or to the assessment of a bill, and the court may make
such order as respects the costs of the assessment as it may think fit."*

6.82. As can be seen, unlike in between the parties assessments where
the decision as to which party will pay the costs is left to the discretion
of the judge, in solicitor client assessments the default provision is that
the costs follow the event:

(i) If the client achieves a reduction to the bill of 20% or more the solicitor will pay the costs of the assessment

(ii) If not, the client will pay the costs

6.83. This is known as 'the one-fifth rule.'

What is the amount of the bill?

6.84. It is surprising how often parties do not agree the amount of the
statute bill. This situation usually arises because the solicitor has discounted the bill. In those circumstances it is essential that the court determine the actual amount of the bill, so that all the parties know the
figure that the one fifth rule applies to.

6.85. *In re Carthew* and *In re Paull*[24] remain authority for how the court
should treat bills that have seemingly been discounted for the purposes
of the one fifth rule.

6.86. In *Carthew* the solicitor delivered a detailed bill consisting of
items amounting to £83 3s. 4d. At the foot of it was written "say £78,".

---

24 (1884) 27 Ch.D. 485

The Court of Appeal found that the meaning of the "but say" figure was:

"Here is my bill for £83 3s. 4d. If you will pay £78 without taxation I will accept it in full discharge. If you do not I will take what taxation gives me."

6.87. The result was that the figure for the purposes of the one fifth rule[25] was £83 not £78.

6.88. In *Paull:*

"The bills as delivered amounted to £361 19s. 2d., but the solicitor stated that he claimed only £320 16s. 6d., which was £41 2s. 8d. less than the amount of the bills. He had previously delivered a cash account in which he had treated the bills as being of the lesser amount. An order for taxation after payment having been obtained, full bills were carried in and the Taxing Master disallowed £81 3s. 8d., reducing their amount to £280 15s. 6d., which is more than five-sixths of the £320 16s."

6.89. Again, the court found that the higher figure was to be used for the purposed of the one fifth rule. The court stated:

"I think it would be exceedingly pernicious to lay down a rule which would enable a solicitor whose bill exceeded what could be allowed on taxation, to oblige his client, by a device of this kind, to have his bill taxed at a greater risk as to costs than if a bill had been delivered for the amount which the solicitor had stated his willingness to accept."

6.90. These cases show that, ordinarily, a solicitor cannot avoid the consequences of the one fifth rule by discounting the statute bill to a lower figure.[26]

---

25 To be precise, at this point in the 19th century it was the "one sixth rule"

26 But see Breyer Group v Prospect Law (2019) Unreported at [72] – [77] where the costs judge found, in the particular circumstances of that case, the lower discounted figure should be used.

Discretion as to costs

6.91. There does remain a discretion to award the costs on a different basis, subject to the judge finding that special circumstances apply. In *Wilsons Solicitor LLP v Bentine*[27] Sales LJ confirmed that the meaning of special circumstances under this part of the Act was the same as under s.70(3) (see Chapter Five).

6.92. For the purposes of the one fifth rule it is the statute bill total (whether a detailed bill or a gross sum bill) which is the relevant figure, not the breakdown. Unless the client has specifically sought to exclude the assessment of certain classes of items under s.70(5) and (6) the whole of the bill is taken into account. It is therefore imperative that a client limits the scope of the assessment if there are types of fees (disbursements for example) which are not in dispute.

6.93. In *Wilsons* the court of appeal considered two questions related to the one fifth rule; firstly, whether costs which are properly considered to be outside the terms of the retainer should be included within the total for the purposes of the one fifth rule and secondly (in the case of *Stone Rowe Brewer v Just Costs Ltd* heard at the same time) whether a costs judge's exercise of discretion as to special circumstances was permissible. The facts are worth considering in both cases.

6.94. In *Wilsons* the solicitors delivered their bill totalling £144,000. Of this sum £7,050 related to costs incurred during a hiatus period (when their client lost capacity) and £24,860 related to fees incurred in respect of the client challenging the amount of the bill.

6.95. The bill was assessed in the sum of £94,000, a reduction of approximately 35%. Surely the client was entitled to have their costs of the assessment as they had comfortably beaten the one fifth rule?

6.96. The costs judge agreed that they should, however, the solicitors appealed arguing that the 'hiatus' costs and the fee challenge costs were outside of the retainer and so should not be taken into account when calculating the total for the purposes of the one fifth rule. If these

---

27 Full citation: Wilson Solicitors LLP v Bentine; Stone Rowe Brewer LLP v Just Costs Ltd [2015] EWCA Civ 1168

charges were removed the reduction was only 16%. There was authority to suggest that this was the proper approach.[28]

6.97. The court of appeal upheld the costs judge's finding:

> "…the costs judge was right to hold that the amount of the overall bill presented by Wilsons was reduced by more than one fifth, so the costs of the assessment should be paid by Wilsons, subject to the exercise of his discretion under section 70(10). There is no good reason to divide up different elements within the bill for the purposes of application of the one fifth rule." [21]

6.98. Thus, where there are elements of the bill that are disallowed on assessment because they do not fall within the retainer these parts will still form the total figure for the purpose of the one fifth rule.

6.99. In the *Stone Rowe Brewer* case the solicitor presented 15 bills of costs totalling £33,000 and both parties agreed that they should be assessed in aggregate. Of these bills five amounted to £20,000 and the client argued that they had no liability for these fees because the solicitor had breached the retainer.

6.100. Just prior to the hearing the parties agreed to settle the bills in the inclusive sum of £23,700 leaving the costs of the assessment to be decided. This was a reduction of approximately 30% and the client sought their costs.

6.101. The solicitor argued that special circumstances existed as the main part of the dispute had been the repudiatory breach argument which would have meant no costs were recovered in relation to those bills. The client had clearly not succeeded on that point.

6.102. The costs judge agreed and allowed the solicitor 70% of their costs on the basis that the repudiatory breach had generated most of the costs and the solicitors were the victors in respect of that argument.

6.103. The court of appeal upheld this decision. Per Sales LJ:

---

28 In re Taxation of Costs; In re A Solicitor [1936] 1 KB 53

"The sort of value judgment which is called for in the context of section 70(10) is one which a costs judge as experienced as Master O'Hare is well-placed to make. When deciding whether "special circumstances" existed, I can see no reason in principle why he should not have had regard to the way in which particular issues arose in the proceedings and the outcome achieved in relation to them. Although I did wonder whether Master O'Hare went too far in describing Just Costs as "the overall victor", and failed thereby to give proper weight to the fact that according to the one fifth rule in section 70(9) SRB was the successful party, I consider on balance that this phraseology does not indicate any error of law or approach on his part. He had specifically reminded himself earlier in his ruling that SRB was the successful party according to the one fifth rule. In applying section 70(10), Master O'Hare was entitled to attach the respective weight that he did to the usual position under the one fifth rule and to the overall outcome for the parties on the issues debated in the proceedings." [70]

6.104. This decision is a good example of where a client can comfortably beat the one fifth rule and still not recover costs.

6.105. A successful offer made in good time in the assessment proceedings can amount to special circumstances. Per Coulson J[29]:

"For the avoidance of doubt, I am in no doubt that a clear without prejudice offer, made in proper time and in proper form, can be a special circumstance which might otherwise reverse the statutory presumption in s 70(9)."

Part 36

6.106. The status of Part 36 offers within assessment proceedings under the Act is not clear. PD46 at 6.19 provides that following assessment the court will:

"(a) complete the court copy of the bill so as to show the amount allowed;

(b) determine the result of the cash account;

29 Angel Airlines SA v Dean & Dean (QBD) - [2009] 2 Costs LR 159 at [25]

(c) award the costs of the detailed assessment hearing in accordance with Section 70(8)[30] of the Solicitors Act 1974; and

(d) issue a final costs certificate."

6.107. As can be seen, the rules expressly provide that the costs of assessment will be determined by the Act itself rather than by reference to Part 36.

6.108. While there is no authority on the point, it would appear that a Part 36 offer is capable of being taken into account as a 'special circumstance' just as any other admissible offer would be. However, on this analysis the party making the offer would not benefit from any of the automatic consequences of an offer being accepted (or judgment being given for a greater amount) as set out in Part 36.

6.109. Perhaps more importantly, if this is correct then CPR r.36.13 does not apply. This provides that upon acceptance of a Part 36 (save where the court considers it unjust to order) the claimant will be entitled to their costs up to the date of acceptance. This deemed costs order is made automatically upon acceptance.

6.110. If the rule does not apply then it is imperative that the offer is made on terms as to costs, otherwise if the offer is accepted there could be an argument that the agreement is silent as to costs. Unless a senior court finds that Part 36 does apply to assessments under the Act it may be safer to simply make a Calderbank offer[31] which provides for payment of one's costs as part of the terms of settlement.

<u>Failure to negotiate</u>

6.111. The failure to negotiate or mediate may also amount to special circumstances. In *Allen v Colman Coyle*[32] Master Simons reduced the solicitor's bill by 14% but found that the solicitor had unreasonably refused to negotiate or agree to mediation. As a result, despite the client not reducing the bill by 20% or more, the judge allowed the solicitor only two thirds of their assessment costs.

---

30 This is a typo in the rules; the rule should read s.70(9)

31 An offer which is headed 'without prejudice save as to costs'

32 [2007] EWHC 90075 (Costs)

CHAPTER SEVEN
ALTERNATIVES TO ASSESSMENTS
UNDER THE ACT

Introduction

7.1. There could be any number of reasons why a solicitor and client may not wish to become involve in formal assessment proceedings. This chapter sets out three alternatives; the first, a complaint to the legal ombudsman is designed to be a quicker and more efficient way of resolving disputes about fees. The second, non-statutory assessments, arises where, for whatever reason, the client cannot bring an action under the Act (for example if they are out of time for commencing an application). There is also the opportunity to mediate solicitor and client disputes.

7.2. Finally, this chapter will look briefly at statutory demands and whether they should ever be used as an alternative to recovery proceedings.

The Legal Ombudsman

7.3. The Legal Ombudsman handles complaints against the entire legal profession, including solicitors. Since this book is about costs (rather than poor service generally) the key question is whether the Ombudsman can consider issues relating to overcharging and what their powers are. The answer is that they can.

7.4. In *Layard Horsfall Ltd v The Legal Ombudsman*[1] the solicitor challenged a decision of the Ombudsman to reduce a fee of £5,000 plus vat to £1,500 plus vat on the basis that the Ombudsman lacked jurisdiction to entertain a complaint in relation to the quantum of fees contractually due. That argument was dismissed and the decision of the Ombudsman was upheld with Phillips J finding:

---

1 [2013] EWHC 4137 (QB)

"…it would be an artificial and unworkable distinction if the Ombudsman could consider the quality and levels of services but not issues of wrongful charging or overcharging." [21]

<u>Who can complain?</u>

7.5. The Scheme Rules[2] provide that the following may use the service:

a) an individual;

b) a business or enterprise that was a micro-enterprise (European Union definition) when it referred the complaint to the authorised person;

c) a charity that had an annual income net of tax of less than £1million when it referred the complaint to the authorised person;

d) a club/association/organisation, the affairs of which are managed by its members/a committee/a committee of its members, that had an annual income net of tax of less than £1 million when it referred the complaint to the authorised person;

e) a trustee of a trust that had an asset value of less than £1million when it referred the complaint to the authorised person;
or

f) a personal representative or beneficiary of the estate of a person who, before he/she died, had not referred the complaint to the Legal Ombudsman.

For (e) and (f) the condition is that the services to which the complaint relates were provided by the respondent to a person –

a) who has subsequently died; and

b) who had not by his or her death referred the complaint to the ombudsman scheme.

7.6. A public body or a legal representative cannot complain to the Ombudsman.

Time Limits

7.7. The client should first try to resolve the dispute with their solicitor. If the client is unsatisfied with the response, or eight weeks has elapsed without a response then a complaint to the Ombudsman may be made.

7.8. However, the Ombudsman may hear a complaint sooner if:

"an ombudsman considers that there are exceptional reasons to consider the complaint sooner, or without it having been made first to the authorised person; or

where an ombudsman considers that in-house resolution is not possible due to irretrievable breakdown in the relationship between an authorised person and the person making the complaint."[3]

7.9. If the response to the complaint includes prominently:

(i) the client's rights to refer the matter to the Ombudsman,

(ii) the contact details of the Ombudsman and

(iii) that there is a time limit of six months from the date of the response

a client ordinarily has six months from the date of the response to bring the complaint.

7.10. The time limit from the date of the action or omission is as follows:

"a) the act or omission, or when the complainant should reasonably have known there was cause for complaint, must have been after 5 October 2010; and

---

3 Scheme Rules 4.2

b) the complainant must refer the complaint to the Legal Ombudsman no later than:

- *six years from the act/omission; or*

- *three years from when the complainant should reasonably have known there was cause for complaint"*[4]

7.11. The Ombudsman may extend the time limits in exceptional circumstances.

Procedure

7.12. The Ombudsman's intention is to respond to complaints within 3 months of receiving the details.

7.13. The complaint will initially be considered by an investigator who will review the matter and explain what the parties could do to resolve the complaint informally. If this is not possible the investigator will issue a preliminary decision and send this to the parties.

7.14. Upon receipt of the preliminary decision the parties will either accept it or reject it. If one or both sides reject it then they should inform the investigator why. The matter is then progressed to an Ombudsman. If both sides accept the decision then the complaint is resolved.

7.15. If there is no response to the preliminary decision the case will be closed (and only re-opened in exceptional circumstances).

7.16. If the preliminary decision is not accepted the matter is passed to an Ombudsman to reconsider the compliant afresh.

Power of the Ombudsman

7.17. The Ombudsman has the power to order the solicitor to:

- Apologise

- Give back any documents that might be needed

---

4 Scheme Rules 4.5

- Put things right

- Refund or reduce the legal fees

- Pay compensation (up to £50,000).

<u>Criteria</u>

7.18. The Ombudsman determines the complaint by reference to what is, in their opinion, fair and reasonable in all the circumstances of the case.

7.19. When considering what is fair and reasonable they will take into account (but not be bound by) the following factors[5]:

a) what decision a court might make;

b) the relevant Approved Regulator's rules of conduct at the time of the act/omission; and

c) what the ombudsman considers to have been good practice at the time of the act/omission.

<u>Fees</u>

7.20. The client pays no fee. The solicitor will pay a fee of £400 unless:

"a) the complaint was:

• abandoned or withdrawn; or

• settled, resolved or determined in favour of the authorised person; and

b) the ombudsman is satisfied that the authorised person took all reasonable steps, under his/her complaints procedures, to try to resolve the complaint."[6]

---

5 Scheme Rules 5.37

6 Scheme Rules 6.2

Enforcement

7.21. A binding and final determination by the Ombudsman can be enforced via the High Court or county court by the client or where appropriate, the Ombudsman itself.

7.22. Where a court enforces a determination it must tell the Ombudsman who:[7]

  a) *will tell the relevant Approved Regulator;*

  b) *may require that Approved Regulator to tell the ombudsman what action it will take; and*

  c) *may report any failure by that Approved Regulator (other than the Claims Management Services Regulator) to the Legal Services Board.*

7.23. The determination may also be published.

Non-Statutory Assessments

7.24. Consider a client who has missed the deadlines under the Act and can no longer have an assessment under s.70. He refuses to pay his bill. His solicitor brings proceedings to recover the fees (or retains the sums from monies on account). Has the client lost all right to challenge the bill?

7.25. The court of appeal considered this question in *Turner & Co (a firm) v O Palomo SA*[8] and held that the right to challenge the fees still remained, even if such a challenge under the Act was no longer possible. Evans LJ cited numerous authorities and held that there was:

> "...*clear Court of Appeal authority for the proposition that a client who is sued by his solicitor for the amount of his charges is entitled to challenge the reasonableness of the sum claimed, notwithstanding that the period during which he may apply for an order for taxation under what is now s 70 of the 1974 Act has expired...Nothing in the Act, or its successors, takes away the need for the solicitor to prove that*

7   Scheme Rules 5.58

8   [1999] 4 All ER 353

his fees are reasonable, if they are challenged, absent any express agreement as to what they should be." [37], [44]

7.26. The court cited with approval Stirling J's explanation of the three ways in which the court can exercise jurisdiction over solicitor's fee:

"Now, in dealing with solicitors' costs, the Court has a three-fold jurisdiction. First, the statutory jurisdiction conferred by the Solicitors Acts ... Secondly, the Court has, I apprehend, jurisdiction to deal with solicitors' bills of costs under its general jurisdiction over the officers of the Court ... Then, thirdly, there remains the ordinary jurisdiction of the Court in dealing with contested claims." [34]

7.27. As can be seen, where the solicitor sues for his fees the court will consider whether they are reasonable in the same way that any claim for damages would be scrutinised. This scrutiny is not avoided simply because the client has lost the right to an assessment under the Act.

7.28. The case of *Ahmud & Co Solicitors v MacPherson*[9] is an example of the procedure likely to be followed where a non-statutory assessment takes place. The solicitors issued Part 7 proceedings to recover costs. A defence was filed accepting that their former client owed costs but no figure was proposed.

7.29. The Master entered judgment for the solicitors for damages to be assessed and then transferred the matter to the SCCO for a non-statutory assessment to be conducted by a costs judge.

7.30. The costs claim was agreed by consent and the parties came before the costs judge only to argue which side should pay the costs of the assessment. The amount agreed was below the one-fifth threshold which would, in an assessment under the Act, ordinarily mean that the client would recover his costs.

7.31. The costs judge determined that the solicitors should pay the costs of the assessment. That order was overturned by Males J, who substituted it for an order that the client pay 75% of the solicitor's costs. The judge commented, obiter, that he considered it wrong to take one part of the Act (the one fifth rule) into account when deciding which party should recover costs in an assessment to which the Act did not apply.

---

9 [2016] 3 Costs LR 443

7.32. However, the judge's conclusion was that the costs judge had been wrong and:

> "...the regime which the Master ought to have applied was that contained in CPR 44.2, the general rule in para 2 of that rule being that the unsuccessful party will be ordered to pay the costs of the successful party, albeit that there is always the possibility of the court making a different order." [24]

7.33. The judge went on:

> "...there were, in my judgment, two errors in the Master's approach which go beyond mere exercise of discretion. I have referred to them both. The first was the rejection of the submission that these proceedings were analogous to an assessment of damages. The second was the Master's view that the client was the successful party. In those circumstances, the Master's exercise of discretion must be set aside."

7.34. If the proceedings were analogous to an assessment of damages then recovery of approx. 80% of the sums sought would clearly signal that the claimant was the successful party. That is what the judge held here. The reduction of the solicitor's costs to 75% reflected for the most part the significant reduction to the fees claimed.

7.35. This case is a good example of why a non-statutory assessment will never be the preferred choice of a client. Nevertheless, it is an important safeguard where the rights under the Act have disappeared.

Mediation

7.36. Disputes between solicitors and their former clients are very often characterised by bad blood. Mediation can be a good way, at an early stage and before significant costs are incurred, of testing whether a settlement is possible.

7.37. If a party suggests mediation in solicitor client proceedings it would be advisable to agree. Failure, without a justifiable reason, to engage with mediation is very likely to result in a costs sanction.

Statutory Demands

7.38. When faced with a client who will not pay their fees, solicitors may be tempted to use a statutory demand. If a demand is served and the debtor does not within 21 days either pay the debt or agree the demand then a winding up petition (in the case of a company owing more than £750) or bankruptcy proceedings (where an individual owes more than £5,000) can be brought against them.

7.39. The service of a statutory demand in respect of solicitor's fees does not fall within s.69 of the Act (which states that no action shall be brought within one month of delivery of the bill) and therefore there is no requirement to wait one month. It can be issued within this period. Per Sir Donald Nicholls V-C[10]:

> "…although 'action' is to be construed liberally I cannot accept that it is wide enough to embrace a non-legal process such as a statutory demand. A statutory demand is one of the statutorily prescribed prerequisites to obtaining remedies afforded to creditors by a bankruptcy order. The demand is not issued by a court…The phrase 'no action shall be brought' is too specific a reference to legal process for that to be a tenable construction."

7.40. A solicitor should however exercise caution. The court will likely set aside a demand where the debtor can show a genuine dispute over the debt. Thus, if the client can legitimately claim that there is a dispute over the bill (and that they wish to have it assessed) the demand will not stand. The solicitor will then have to meet the costs.

7.41. The further complication for solicitors is whether the bill (if it has not been assessed) is a liquidated sum. If it is not then a demand should not be issued. In all but the most basic fixed fee agreements (where there is no possibility of the sum being reduced on assessment) it is difficult to see how such a bill could be a liquidated sum.

7.42. To conclude, ordinarily issuing a statutory demand whilst superficially attractive will not be appropriate. It may result in the solicitor paying the costs of setting it aside.

---

10 Re a debtor (No 88 of 1991) – [1992] 4 All ER 301 at 305

APPENDIX A
EXCERPTS FROM THE SOLICITORS
ACT 1974 (AS AMENDED)

S.57. Non–contentious business agreements

(1) Whether or not any order is in force under section 56, a solicitor and his client may, before or after or in the course of the transaction of any non–contentious business by the solicitor, make an agreement as to his remuneration in respect of that business.

(2) The agreement may provide for the remuneration of the solicitor by a gross sum or by reference to an hourly rate, or by a commission or percentage, or by a salary, or otherwise, and it may be made on the terms that the amount of the remuneration stipulated for shall or shall not include all or any disbursements made by the solicitor in respect of searches, plans, travelling, taxes , fees or other matters.

(3) The agreement shall be in writing and signed by the person to be bound by it or his agent in that behalf.

(4) Subject to subsections (5) and (7), the agreement may be sued and recovered on or set aside in the like manner and on the like grounds as an agreement not relating to the remuneration of a solicitor.

(5) If on any assessment of costs the agreement is relied on by the solicitor and objected to by the client as unfair or unreasonable, the costs officer may enquire into the facts and certify them to the court, and if from that certificate it appears just to the court that the agreement should be set aside, or the amount payable under it reduced, the court may so order and may give such consequential directions as it thinks fit.

(6) Subsection (7) applies where the agreement provides for the remuneration of the solicitor to be by reference to an hourly rate.

(7) If, on the assessment of any costs, the agreement is relied on by the solicitor and the client objects to the amount of the costs (but is not al-

leging that the agreement is unfair or unreasonable), the costs officer may enquire into—

(a) the number of hours worked by the solicitor; and

(b) whether the number of hours worked by him was excessive.]

S.59. Contentious business agreements

(1) Subject to subsection (2), a solicitor may make an agreement in writing with his client as to his remuneration in respect of any contentious business done, or to be done, by him (in this Act referred to as a "contentious business agreement") providing that he shall be remunerated by a gross sum or by reference to an hourly rate, or by a salary, or otherwise, and whether at a higher or lower rate than that at which he would otherwise have been entitled to be remunerated.

(2) Nothing in this section or in sections 60 to 63 shall give validity to —

(a) any purchase by a solicitor of the interest, or any part of the interest, of his client in any action, suit or other contentious proceeding; or

(b) any agreement by which a solicitor retained or employed to prosecute any action, suit or other contentious proceeding, stipulates for payment only in the event of success in that action, suit or proceeding; or

(c) any disposition, contract, settlement, conveyance, delivery, dealing or transfer which under the law relating to bankruptcy is invalid against a trustee or creditor in any bankruptcy or composition.

S.65. Security for costs and termination of retainer

(1) A solicitor may take security from his client for his costs, to be ascertained by assessment or otherwise, in respect of any contentious business to be done by him.

(2) If a solicitor who has been retained by a client to conduct contentious business requests the client to make a payment of a sum of money, being a reasonable sum on account of the costs incurred or to be in-

curred in the conduct of that business and the client refuses or fails within a reasonable time to make that payment, the refusal or failure shall be deemed to be a good cause whereby the solicitor may, upon giving reasonable notice to the client, withdraw from the retainer.

S.67. Inclusion of disbursements in bill of costs

A solicitor's bill of costs may include costs payable in discharge of a liability properly incurred by him on behalf of the party to be charged with the bill (including counsel's fees) notwithstanding that those costs have not been paid before the delivery of the bill to that party; but those costs—

(a) shall be described in the bill as not then paid; and

(b) if the bill is assessed, shall not be allowed by the costs officer unless they are paid before the assessment is completed.

S.68. Power of court to order solicitor to deliver bill, etc

(1) The jurisdiction of the High Court to make orders for the delivery by a solicitor of a bill of costs, and for the delivery up of, or otherwise in relation to, any documents in his possession, custody or power, is hereby declared to extend to cases in which no business has been done by him in the High Court.

(2) The county court and the family court each have the same jurisdiction as the High Court to make orders making such provision as is mentioned in subsection (1) in cases where the bill of costs or the documents relate wholly or partly to contentious business done by the solicitor in the county court or (as the case may be) the family court.

(3) In this section and in sections 69 to 71 "solicitor" includes the executors, administrators and assignees of a solicitor.

S.69. Action to recover solicitor's costs

(1) Subject to the provisions of this Act, no action shall be brought to recover any costs due to a solicitor before the expiration of one month from the date on which a bill of those costs is delivered in accordance

with the requirements mentioned in subsection (2); but if there is probable cause for believing that the party chargeable with the costs—

(a) is about to quit England and Wales, to become bankrupt or to compound with his creditors, or

(b) is about to do any other act which would tend to prevent or delay the solicitor obtaining payment, the High Court may, notwithstanding that one month has not expired from the delivery of the bill, order that the solicitor be at liberty to commence an action to recover his costs and may order that those costs be assessed.

(2) The requirements referred to in subsection (1) are that the bill must be—

(a) signed in accordance with subsection (2A), and

(b) delivered in accordance with subsection (2C).

(2A) A bill is signed in accordance with this subsection if it is—

(a) signed by the solicitor or on his behalf by an employee of the solicitor authorised by him to sign, or

(b) enclosed in, or accompanied by, a letter which is signed as mentioned in paragraph (a) and refers to the bill.

(2B) For the purposes of subsection (2A) the signature may be an electronic signature.

(2C) A bill is delivered in accordance with this subsection if—

(a) it is delivered to the party to be charged with the bill personally,

(b) it is delivered to that party by being sent to him by post to, or left for him at, his place of business, dwelling-house or last known place of abode, or

(c) it is delivered to that party—

(i) by means of an electronic communications network, or

(ii) by other means but in a form that nevertheless requires the use of apparatus by the recipient to render it intelligible, and that party has indicated to the person making the delivery his willingness to accept delivery of a bill sent in the form and manner used.

(2D) An indication to any person for the purposes of subsection (2C)(c) —

(a) must state the address to be used and must be accompanied by such other information as that person requires for the making of the delivery;

(b) may be modified or withdrawn at any time by a notice given to that person.

(2E) Where a bill is proved to have been delivered in compliance with the requirements of subsections (2A) and (2C), it is not necessary in the first instance for the solicitor to prove the contents of the bill and it is to be presumed, until the contrary is shown, to be a bill bona fide complying with this Act.

(2F) A bill which is delivered as mentioned in subsection (2C)(c) is to be treated as having been delivered on the first working day after the day on which it was sent (unless the contrary is proved).

(3) Where a bill of costs relates wholly or partly to contentious business done in the county court and the amount of the bill does not exceed £5,000, the powers and duties of the High Court under this section and sections 70 and 71 in relation to that bill may be exercised and performed by the county court.

(5) In this section references to an electronic signature are to be read in accordance with section 7(2) of the Electronic Communications Act 2000 (c. 7).

(6) In this section—

"electronic communications network" has the same meaning as in the Communications Act 2003 (c. 21);

"working day" means a day other than a Saturday, a Sunday, Christmas Day, Good Friday or a bank holiday in England and Wales under the Banking and Financial Dealings Act 1971 (c. 80).

S.70. Assessment on application of party chargeable or solicitor

(1) Where before the expiration of one month from the delivery of a solicitor's bill an application is made by the party chargeable with the bill, the High Court shall, without requiring any sum to be paid into court, order that the bill be assessed and that no action be commenced on the bill until the assessment is completed.

(2) Where no such application is made before the expiration of the period mentioned in subsection (1), then, on an application being made by the solicitor or, subject to subsections (3) and (4), by the party chargeable with the bill, the court may on such terms, if any, as it thinks fit (not being terms as to the costs of the assessment), order—

(a) that the bill be assessed; and

(b) that no action be commenced on the bill, and that any action already commenced be stayed, until the assessment is completed.

(3) Where an application under subsection (2) is made by the party chargeable with the bill—

(a) after the expiration of 12 months from the delivery of the bill, or

(b) after a judgment has been obtained for the recovery of the costs covered by the bill, or

(c) after the bill has been paid, but before the expiration of 12 months from the payment of the bill.no order shall be made except in special circumstances and, if an order is made, it may contain such terms as regards the costs of the assessment as the court may think fit.

(4) The power to order assessment conferred by subsection (2) shall not be exercisable on an application made by the party chargeable with the bill after the expiration of 12 months from the payment of the bill.

(5) An order for the assessment of a bill made on an application under this section by the party chargeable with the bill shall, if he so requests, be an order for the assessment of the profit costs covered by the bill.

(6) Subject to subsection (5), the court may under this section order the assessment of all the costs, or of the profit costs, or of the costs other than profit costs and, where part of the costs is not to be assessed, may allow an action to be commenced or to be continued for that part of the costs.

(7) Every order for the assessment of a bill shall require the costs officer to assess not only the bill but also the costs of the assessment and to certify what is due to or by the solicitor in respect of the bill and in respect of the costs of the taxation.

(8) If after due notice of any assessment either party to it fails to attend, the officer may proceed with the assessment ex parte.

(9) Unless—

(a) the order for assessment was made on the application of the solicitor and the party chargeable does not attend the assessment , or

(b) the order for assessment or an order under subsection (10) otherwise provides, the costs of an assessment shall be paid according to the event of the assessment, that is to say, if the amount of the bill is reduced by one fifth, the solicitor shall pay the costs, but otherwise the party chargeable shall pay the costs.

(10) The costs officer may certify to the court any special circumstances relating to a bill or to the assessment of a bill, and the court may make such order as respects the costs of the assessment as it may think fit.

(12) In this section "profit costs" means costs other than counsel's fees or costs paid or payable in the discharge of a liability incurred by the solicitor on behalf of the party chargeable, and the reference in subsection (9) to the fraction of the amount of the reduction in the bill shall be taken, where the assessment concerns only part of the costs covered by the bill, as a reference to that fraction of the amount of those costs which is being assessed.

S.71. Assessment on application of third parties

(1) Where a person other than the party chargeable with the bill for the purposes of section 70 has paid, or is or was liable to pay, a bill either to the solicitor or to the party chargeable with the bill, that person, or his executors, administrators or assignees may apply to the High Court for an order for the assessment of the bill as if he were the party chargeable with it, and the court may make the same order (if any) as it might have made if the application had been made by the party chargeable with the bill.

(2) Where the court has no power to make an order by virtue of subsection (1) except in special circumstances it may, in considering whether there are special circumstances sufficient to justify the making of an order, take into account circumstances which affect the applicant but do not affect the party chargeable with the bill.

(3) Where a trustee, executor or administrator has become liable to pay a bill of a solicitor, then, on the application of any person interested in any property out of which the trustee, executor or administrator has paid, or is entitled to pay, the bill, the court may order—

(a) that the bill be assessed on such terms, if any, as it thinks fit; and

(b) that such payments, in respect of the amount found to be due to or by the solicitor and in respect of the costs of the assessment, be made to or by the applicant, to or by the solicitor, or to or by the executor, administrator or trustee, as it thinks fit.

(4) In considering any application under subsection (3) the court shall have regard—

(a) to the provisions of section 70 as to applications by the party chargeable for the assessment of a solicitor's bill so far as they are capable of being applied to an application made under that subsection;

(b) to the extent and nature of the interest of the applicant.

(5) If an applicant under subsection (3) pays any money to the solicitor, he shall have the same right to be paid that money by the trustee, executor or administrator chargeable with the bill as the solicitor had.

(6) Except in special circumstances, no order shall be made on an application under this section for the assessment of a bill which has already been assessed.

(7) If the court on an application under this section orders a bill to be assessed, it may order the solicitor to deliver to the applicant a copy of the bill on payment of the costs of that copy.

S.74. Special provisions as to contentious business done in county courts

(1) The remuneration of a solicitor in respect of contentious business done by him in [the county court] shall be regulated in accordance with sections 59 to 73, and for that purpose those sections shall have effect subject to the following provisions of this section.

(3) The amount which may be allowed on the assessment of any costs or bill of costs in respect of any item relating to proceedings in the county court shall not, except in so far as rules of court may otherwise provide, exceed the amount which could have been allowed in respect of that item as between party and party in those proceedings, having regard to the nature of the proceedings and the amount of the claim and of any counterclaim.

APPENDIX B
SELECTED CIVIL PROCEDURE RULES

Basis of detailed assessment of solicitor and client costs

46.9

(1) This rule applies to every assessment of a solicitor's bill to a client except a bill which is to be paid out of the Community Legal Service Fund under the Legal Aid Act 1988 or the Access to Justice Act 1999 or by the Lord Chancellor under Part 1 of the Legal Aid, Sentencing and Punishment of Offenders Act 2012.

(2) Section 74(3) of the Solicitors Act 1974 applies unless the solicitor and client have entered into a written agreement which expressly permits payment to the solicitor of an amount of costs greater than that which the client could have recovered from another party to the proceedings.

(3) Subject to paragraph (2), costs are to be assessed on the indemnity basis but are to be presumed -

(a) to have been reasonably incurred if they were incurred with the express or implied approval of the client;

(b) to be reasonable in amount if their amount was expressly or impliedly approved by the client;

(c) to have been unreasonably incurred if –

(i) they are of an unusual nature or amount; and

(ii) the solicitor did not tell the client that as a result the costs might not be recovered from the other party.

(4) Where the court is considering a percentage increase on the application of the client, the court will have regard to all the relevant factors as

they reasonably appeared to the solicitor or counsel when the conditional fee agreement was entered into or varied.

Assessment procedure

46.10

(1) This rule sets out the procedure to be followed where the court has made an order under Part III of the Solicitors Act 1974 for the assessment of costs payable to a solicitor by the solicitor's client.

(2) The solicitor must serve a breakdown of costs within 28 days of the order for costs to be assessed.

(3) The client must serve points of dispute within 14 days after service on the client of the breakdown of costs.

(4) The solicitor must serve any reply within 14 days of service on the solicitor of the points of dispute.

(5) Either party may file a request for a hearing date –

(a) after points of dispute have been served; but

(b) no later than 3 months after the date of the order for the costs to be assessed.

(6) This procedure applies subject to any contrary order made by the court.

46PD

Assessment of solicitor and client costs: rules 46.9 and 46.10

6.1 A client and solicitor may agree whatever terms they consider appropriate about the payment of the solicitor's charges. If however, the costs are of an unusual nature, either in amount or the type of costs incurred, those costs will be presumed to have been unreasonably incurred unless the solicitor satisfies the court that the client was informed that they were unusual and that they might not be allowed on an assessment of costs between the parties. That information must have been given to the client before the costs were incurred.

6.2 Costs as between a solicitor and client are assessed on the indemnity basis. The presumptions in rule 46.9(3) are rebuttable.

6.3 If a party fails to comply with the requirements of rule 46.10 concerning the service of a breakdown of costs or points of dispute, any other party may apply to the court in which the detailed assessment hearing should take place for an order requiring compliance. If the court makes such an order, it may –

(a) make it subject to conditions including a condition to pay a sum of money into court; and

(b) specify the consequence of failure to comply with the order or a condition.

6.4 The procedure for obtaining an order under Part III of the Solicitors Act 1974 is by a Part 8 claim, as modified by rule 67.3 and Practice Direction 67. Precedent J of the Schedule of Costs Precedents is a model form of claim form. The application must be accompanied by the bill or bills in respect of which assessment is sought, and, if the claim concerns a conditional fee agreement, a copy of that agreement. If the original bill is not available a copy will suffice.

6.5 Model forms of order, which the court may make, are set out in Precedents K, L and M of the Schedule of Costs Precedents.

6.6 The breakdown of costs referred to in rule 46.10 is a document which contains the following information –

(a) details of the work done under each of the bills sent for assessment; and

(b) in applications under Section 70 of the Solicitors Act 1974, a cash account showing money received by the solicitor to the credit of the client and sums paid out of that money on behalf of the client but not payments out which were made in satisfaction of the bill or of any items which are claimed in the bill.

6.7 Precedent P of the Schedule of Costs Precedents is a model form of breakdown of costs. A party who is required to serve a breakdown of costs must also serve –

(a) copies of the fee notes of counsel and of any expert in respect of fees claimed in the breakdown, and

(b) written evidence as to any other disbursement which is claimed in the breakdown and which exceeds £250.

6.8 The provisions relating to default costs certificates (rule 47.11) do not apply to cases to which rule 46.10 applies.

6.9 The time for requesting a detailed assessment hearing is within 3 months after the date of the order for the costs to be assessed.

6.10 The form of request for a hearing date must be in Form N258C. The request must be accompanied by copies of –

(a) the order sending the bill or bills for assessment;

(b) the bill or bills sent for assessment;

(c) the solicitor's breakdown of costs and any invoices or accounts served with that breakdown;

(d) a copy of the points of dispute;

(e) a copy of any replies served;

(f) a statement signed by the party filing the request or that party's legal representative giving the names and addresses for service of all parties to the proceedings.

6.11 The request must include the estimated length of hearing.

6.12 On receipt of the request the court will fix a date for the hearing, or will give directions.

6.13 The court will give at least 14 days notice of the time and place of the detailed assessment hearing.

6.14 Unless the court gives permission, only the solicitor whose bill it is and parties who have served points of dispute may be heard and only items specified in the points of dispute may be raised.

6.15 If a party wishes to vary that party's breakdown of costs, points of dispute or reply, an amended or supplementary document must be filed with the court and copies of it must be served on all other relevant parties. Permission is not required to vary a breakdown of costs, points of dispute or a reply but the court may disallow the variation or permit it only upon conditions, including conditions as to the payment of any costs caused or wasted by the variation.

6.16 Unless the court directs otherwise the solicitor must file with the court the papers in support of the bill not less than 7 days before the date for the detailed assessment hearing and not more than 14 days before that date.

6.17 Once the detailed assessment hearing has ended it is the responsibility of the legal representative appearing for the solicitor or, as the case may be, the solicitor in person to remove the papers filed in support of the bill.

6.18 If, in the course of a detailed assessment hearing of a solicitor's bill to that solicitor's client, it appears to the court that in any event the solicitor will be liable in connection with that bill to pay money to the client, it may issue an interim certificate specifying an amount which in its opinion is payable by the solicitor to the client.

6.19 After the detailed assessment hearing is concluded the court will –

(a) complete the court copy of the bill so as to show the amount allowed;

(b) determine the result of the cash account;

(c) award the costs of the detailed assessment hearing in accordance with Section 70(8) of the Solicitors Act 1974; and

(d) issue a final costs certificate.

Proceedings relating to solicitors

67

Scope and interpretation

67.1

(1) This Part contains rules about the following types of proceedings relating to solicitors –

(a) proceedings to obtain an order for a solicitor to deliver a bill or cash account and proceedings in relation to money or papers received by a solicitor (rule 67.2);

(b) proceedings under Part III of the Solicitors Act 1974 relating to the remuneration of solicitors (rule 67.3); and

(c) proceedings under Schedule 1 to the Solicitors Act 1974 arising out of the Law Society's intervention in a solicitor's practice (rule 67.4).

Power to order solicitor to deliver cash account etc.

67.2

(1) Where the relationship of solicitor and client exists or has existed, the orders which the court may make against the solicitor, on the application of the client or his personal representatives, include any of the following –

(a) to deliver a bill or cash account;

(b) to pay or deliver up any money or securities;

(c) to deliver a list of the moneys or securities which the solicitor has in his possession or control on behalf of the applicant;

(d) to pay into or lodge in court any such money or securities.

(2) An application for an order under this rule must be made –

(a) by Part 8 claim form; or

(b) if the application is made in existing proceedings, by application notice in accordance with Part 23.

(3) If the solicitor alleges that he has a claim for costs against the applicant, the court may make an order for –

(a) the detailed assessment and payment of those costs; and

(b) securing the payment of the costs, or protecting any solicitor's lien.

Proceedings under Part III of the Act

67.3

(1) A claim for an order under Part III of the Act for the assessment of costs payable to a solicitor by his client –

(a) which –

(i) relates to contentious business done in a county court; and

(ii) is within the financial limit of the County Court's jurisdiction specified in section 69(3) of the Act,

may be made in the County Court;

(b) in every other case, must be made in the High Court.

(Rule 30.2 makes provision for the County Court to transfer the proceedings to another county court for detailed assessment of costs)

(Provisions about the venue for detailed assessment proceedings are contained in rule 47.4 and paragraphs 4.1 to 4.3 of Practice Direction 47)

(2) A claim for an order under Part III of the Act must be made –

(a) by Part 8 claim form; or

(b) if the claim is made in existing proceedings, by application notice in accordance with Part 23.

(A model form of claim form is annexed to the Costs Practice Direction)

(3) A claim in the High Court under Part III of the Act may be determined by –

(a) a High Court judge;

(b) a Master, a costs judge or a District Judge of the Principal Registry of the Family Division; or

(c) a District Judge, if the costs are for –

(i) contentious business done in proceedings in the District Registry of which he is the District Judge;

(ii) contentious business done in proceedings in the County Court within the district of that District Registry; or

(iii) non-contentious business.

Proceedings under Schedule 1 to the Act

67.4

(1) Proceedings in the High Court under Schedule 1 to the Act must be brought –

(a) in the Chancery Division; and

(b) by Part 8 claim form, unless paragraph (4) below applies.

(2) The heading of the claim form must state that the claim relates to a solicitor and is made under Schedule 1 to the Act.

(3) Where proceedings are brought under paragraph 6(4) or 9(8) of Schedule 1 to the Act, the court will give directions and fix a date for the hearing immediately upon issuing the claim form.

(4) If the court has made an order under Schedule 1 to the Act, any subsequent application for an order under that Schedule which has the same parties may be made by a Part 23 application in the same proceedings.

PD67

General

1 This Practice Direction applies to proceedings under Rule 67.2 and to the following types of claim under Rule 67.3 and Part III of the Solicitors Act 1974 ('the Act'):

(1) an application under section 57(5) of the Act for a costs officer to enquire into the facts and certify whether a non-contentious business agreement should be set aside or the amount payable under it reduced;

(2) a claim under section 61(1) of the Act for the court to enforce or set aside a contentious business agreement and determine questions as to its validity and effect;

(3) a claim by a client under s 61(3) of the Act for a costs officer to examine a contentious business agreement as to its fairness and reasonableness;

(4) where the amount agreed under a contentious business agreement has been paid, a claim under section 61(5) of the Act for the agreement to be re-opened and the costs assessed;

(5) proceedings under section 62 of the Act for the examination of a contentious business agreement, where the client makes the agreement as a representative of a person whose property will be chargeable with the amount payable;

(6) proceedings under section 63 of the Act where, after some business has been done under a contentious business agreement, but before the solicitor has wholly performed it:

(a) the solicitor dies or becomes incapable of acting; or

(b) the client changes solicitor;

(7) where an action is commenced on a gross sum bill, an application under section 64(3) of the Act for an order that the bill be assessed;

(8) a claim under section 68 of the Act for the delivery by a solicitor of a bill of costs and for the delivery up of, or otherwise in relation to, any documents;

(9) an application under section 69 of the Act for an order that the solicitor be at liberty to commence an action to recover his costs within one month of delivery of the bill;

(10) a claim under section 70(1) of the Act, by the party chargeable with the solicitor's bill, for an order that the bill be assessed and that no action be taken on the bill until the assessment is completed;

(11) a claim under section 70(2) of the Act, by either party, for an order that the bill be assessed and that no action be commenced or continued on the bill until the assessment is completed;

(12) a claim under section 70(3) of the Act, by the party chargeable with the bill, for detailed assessment showing special circumstances;

(13) a claim under section 71(1) of the Act, by a person other than the party chargeable with the bill, for detailed assessment;

(14) a claim under section 71(3) of the Act, by any person interested in any property out of which a trustee, executor or administrator has paid or is entitled to pay a solicitor's bill, for detailed assessment; and

(15) a claim by a solicitor under section 73 of the Act for a charging order.

Proceedings in the costs office

2.1 Where a claim to which this practice direction applies is made by Part 8 claim form in the High Court in London –

(1) if the claim is of a type referred to in paragraphs 1(1) to (5), it must be issued in the Costs Office;

(2) in any other case, the claim may be issued in the Costs Office.

2.2 A claim which is made by Part 8 claim form in a district registry or by Part 23 application notice in existing High Court proceedings may be referred to the Costs Office.

2.2A Where a claim under section 70 or 71 of the Act is made by Part 8 claim form in the Costs Office, the court will fix a date for a hearing at which directions will be given, unless the claim is not contested, when an order for detailed assessment will be made. Evidence need not be filed or served by either party before that hearing.

2.3 'Costs Office' has the same meaning as set out in rule 44.1(1).

Evidence in proceedings for order for detailed assessment

4 Where a Part 8 claim is brought for an order for the detailed assessment of a solicitor's bill of costs, the parties are not required to comply with Rule 8.5 unless:

(1) the claim will be contested; or

(2) the court directs that the parties should comply with Rule 8.5.

MORE BOOKS BY
LAW BRIEF PUBLISHING

A selection of our other titles available now:-

'Covid-19, Homeworking and the Law – The Essential Guide to Employment and GDPR Issues' by Forbes Solicitors
'Covid-19, Force Majeure and Frustration of Contracts – The Essential Guide' by Keith Markham
'Covid-19 and Criminal Law – The Essential Guide' by Ramya Nagesh
'Covid-19 and Family Law in England and Wales – The Essential Guide' by Safda Mahmood
'Covid-19 and the Implications for Planning Law – The Essential Guide' by Bob Mc Geady & Meyric Lewis
'Covid-19, Residential Property, Equity Release and Enfranchisement – The Essential Guide' by Paul Sams and Louise Uphill
'Covid-19, Brexit and the Law of Commercial Leases – The Essential Guide' by Mark Shelton
'Covid-19 and the Law Relating to Food in the UK and Republic of Ireland – The Essential Guide' by Ian Thomas
'A Practical Guide to the General Data Protection Regulation (GDPR) – 2nd Edition' by Keith Markham
'Ellis on Credit Hire – Sixth Edition' by Aidan Ellis & Tim Kevan
'A Practical Guide to Working with Litigants in Person and McKenzie Friends in Family Cases' by Stuart Barlow
'Protecting Unregistered Brands: A Practical Guide to the Law of Passing Off' by Lorna Brazell
'A Practical Guide to Secondary Liability and Joint Enterprise Post-Jogee' by Joanne Cecil & James Mehigan

'A Practical Guide to Chronic Pain Claims' by Pankaj Madan

'A Practical Guide to Claims Arising from Fatal Accidents' by James Patience

'A Practical Guide to Subtle Brain Injury Claims' by Pankaj Madan

These books and more are available to order online direct from the publisher at www.lawbriefpublishing.com, where you can also read free sample chapters. For any queries, contact us on 0844 587 2383 or mail@lawbriefpublishing.com.

Our books are also usually in stock at www.amazon.co.uk with free next day delivery for Prime members, and at good legal bookshops such as Wildy & Sons.

We are regularly launching new books in our series of practical day-to-day practitioners' guides. Visit our website and join our free newsletter to be kept informed and to receive special offers, free chapters, etc.

You can also follow us on Twitter at www.twitter.com/lawbriefpub.

Lightning Source UK Ltd.
Milton Keynes UK
UKHW022150150621
385567UK00005B/138

9 781913 715397